BETH QUINN

UNLEASHED

The Collected Dog Columns

Grandpup Gus 1998

Brigette Olejniczak

ROYAL FIREWORKS PRESS

UNIONVILLE, NEW YORK

Except where otherwise noted, all photography by **Beth Quinn**
Layout and design by **Mimi Estes**

On the Front and Back Cover
Tom and Huck Quinn

Royal Fireworks Press
First Ave, PO Box 399
Unionville NY 10988
845 726 4444
Fax 845 726 3824
Email: mail@rfwp.com
Website: rfwp.com

ISBN: 978-0-8802-973-8 [0-88092-973-1]

Printed and bound in the United States of America by American citizens using recycled, acid-free paper, vegetable-based inks, and environmentally-friendly cover coatings at the
Royal Fireworks Printing Company of Unionville, New York.

Phil Kamrass

For Scout, the little brown dog
1991-2003

*And for all the other dogs who have given their hearts
to our family and asked so little in return:*

Mike, Rusty and Missy – the dogs of my childhood

*Molly, Cassidy, Max, Riley, Huck and Tom –
the dogs of my adulthood*

Jack, Gus, Hank and Little Mac – the grandpups

*Thank you for the laughter, the love
and the enormous good cheer in all weather.*

Heaven goes by favor.
If it went by merit, you would stay out
and your dog would go in.

– Mark Twain

Contents

Preface

Last night, when I got home from work, I couldn't find Tom.

Normally, he greets me at the door, right along with his pal Huckleberry. But only Huck was at the door last night.

I set out in search of my loopy yellow Lab, which took all of a minute. My house is small, and Tom is big. But no Tom materialized. Not asleep on a bed, not in the basement, not on the porch.

I went into the yard and called for him. He and Huck have a dog door leading to the back yard, so I thought perhaps I'd arrived home at an awkward time for him. Maybe he was in the middle of his twice-daily constitutional (wouldn't you LOVE to be that regular?) and didn't want to interrupt what was likely the most satisfying moment of his day just to greet me at the door.

But no Tom.

I was suddenly very scared. Could he somehow have escaped from our fenced-in yard and gotten lost? He's not all that good at directions. He could get lost going next door.

I returned to the house and stood in the kitchen, trying to stave off the panic. At 2, Tom is only a baby. He will always be only a baby.

Huck, at 2½, is largely responsible for him. She walks him by holding his leash in her mouth, and she supervises him when my husband and I are at work. This primarily involves mapping out Tom's day for him (breakfast, nap, pee, run, bark, pee, nap, bark and so on – it's a complicated schedule).

Perhaps unfairly, I was inclined to blame Huck for his disappearance.

"Where IS he!" I demanded. "You were supposed to watch him."

Huck sat down and started nibbling at a fingernail. Well, what did I expect?

It was then that I heard Tom crying. Relief washed over me. He was here! Somewhere. But where?

I searched again, this time more thoroughly. Under the beds, in the bathtub, in the closets.

Finally, I went all the way into the living room – a room I'd given only a cursory glance the first time through. And there, on the 15-inch-wide bay window ledge, was Tom.

He was a wreck. So were the curtains.

He'd apparently climbed up onto the ledge from the couch, but then found the area too narrow to turn around for a retreat. It has never occurred to me to teach him to walk backwards. I thought dogs just picked up that kind of skill from being dogs. Not Tom.

And it never occurred to him to jump down. It's only three

feet off the floor. He practically could have stepped down. But he didn't cogitate that particular thought.

Who knows how long he'd been there? All day, perhaps, and I only assume this based on how pleased he was to get outside and relieve himself for a full 90 seconds. That boy has a fine bladder.

So this is my world and has been for most of my life. I have, by virtue of fate – or poor training skills – always been in the company of confused, confounded, cowardly, crazy, costly dogs.

I began writing occasional columns about them in the Times Herald-Record in 1984. When I first got the idea for this book, I was shocked to discover that I've written nearly 50 columns about my various dogs over the years.

What's even more shocking is that readers – those, at least, who have their own mixed-up lives with dogs – continue to read them. It's not uncommon for people I meet for the first time to ask after the dogs' health. "So, how are Huck and Tom?" they want to know. No one ever asks how my husband and kids are.

Even readers who just hate my political columns seem to like the dogs. I got an e-mail from a man a few weeks ago who took strong exception to my criticism of George Bush. After taking issue with my opinions, my looks and my morals, he ended by saying, "Even Huck writes better than you do!!!!"

Take that! I wonder if he thought Huck actually writes her own stuff.

I'm told that it costs, on average, $6,400 to raise a medium-sized dog to the age of 11. I think that's a low estimate myself. It's a fortune just keeping my dogs supplied with Greenies, which they snuffle up like it's heroin.

That's why I'm grateful you bought this book. My Greenie supplier has a comfortable lifestyle, and I'm responsible for keeping him in the manner to which he's grown accustomed.

And so, I just want to say thank you.

Thank you for reading my columns over the years, and for asking about the dogs when we meet.

Thank you for grieving with me when we lost Scout.

Thank you for laughing with me when one or another of our dogs has pranced across the Record's pages in pursuit of some dopey dogly derring-do.

And thank you for getting a kick out of dogs – both yours and mine.

You're the best.

Beth Quinn
October 2005

Rusty c. 1966

'*Our plan to see sex was straightforward and simple.
We would hold a boy dog and a lady dog prisoner
in the farm's hayloft, and then watch until they
developed an attraction for one another
and did some sex with us as an audience.*'

The Birds and the Bees in the Dog Days of Summer

I was 10 years old the summer my friend Gigi and I decided we should see some sex.

We had never seen sex, and no one seemed inclined to describe it to us. We had only a vague notion as to what it was for, and an even vaguer notion as to the rudiments of the event.

We knew only that it was something done between a man and a lady, and that animals did it, too. It was Gigi who supplied that last bit of intelligence, as she had older cousins who lived on the farm behind our house, and she'd heard them talking about it that summer while she was there for a visit.

Our plan to see sex was straightforward and simple. We would hold a boy dog and a lady dog prisoner in the farm's hayloft, and then watch until they developed an attraction for one another and did some sex with us as an audience.

We were somewhat limited, though, as to choice of dog. For the lady, we picked the only female available – a big, red Irish setter named Dinah, belonging to Gigi's cousins. Dinah was a tall dog who must have weighed about 90 pounds. She had an aristocratic manner, and so we were anxious to find her a suitable boyfriend.

Unfortunately, the only boy dog we could convince to participate in our plan was a little Beagle-mix by the name of Rusty. Rusty was a town dog, and no one was sure where he'd come from. He'd just shown up one day, and he took turns living with families on our street. It was our turn that week, so Rusty was our man.

The fact that he was a squat 30 pounds disturbed Gigi and me somewhat, but it was the best we could come up with on short notice.

There were several obstacles to surmount, though, before we could see some sex.

Our major challenge was getting the dogs into the hayloft. The only entrance was by stepladder, and neither dog showed any acumen for climbing the thing. Rusty tried, I'll give him that. But he couldn't get his hind legs to follow after his front ones.

Gigi, who was the brains of the outfit, finally hit on the plan to hoist the dogs up on a pulley we designed out of an inverted horse saddle. We strapped them in, one at a time, and hauled them up with the winch that was normally used to pull up hay bales.

Dinah didn't like it much, but Rusty, who was always game for a new adventure, thought it was a fine arrangement. He liked the loft, too, although it was too dusty and closed-in smelling for Dinah's taste.

The dogs didn't seem inclined to do some sex straight off, though – in fact Dinah seemed pretty haughty at the suggestion – and Gigi and I realized early on that we would have to give them some time to get acquainted. So we set about the task of laying in some supplies to last us however long it took.

We toted food and water, sleeping bags and lanterns, books and dog biscuits, and every other necessity we could think of, including a brush we planned to use on Rusty to improve his looks and make him more attractive to Dinah. It took all of an afternoon to get settled up there in preparation to see some sex.

By nightfall we were ready. So was Rusty. He was the most gallant little dog there ever was. He tried every which way to attract Dinah's notice, but Dinah spurned his every advance.

Watching his efforts, it finally occurred to us that their height difference might be posing something of a problem for Rusty, so I went down the ladder to find something that might help him out in that regard. I brought back a wooden crate for Rusty to stand on, and he seemed appreciative.

But it all proved to be a waste of effort. Dinah was a snob and a man-hater to boot, and no amount of cajolery or hair brushing or wooden crates was going to soften her heart toward Rusty.

We finally gave it up around midnight. We lowered Dinah to the ground floor in the inverted saddle, and she ran off for a sulk.

Gigi and I crawled into our sleeping bags and shared a bag of popcorn and a bottle of soda. I opened up "The Bobbsey Twins at the Seashore," she opened her Hardy Boys adventure, and Rusty curled up between us for the night.

The Dog Who Was Hit by the Mob

When I was a kid, my dog Mike was taken out by the mob.

By the 16-year-old son of a local mobster, actually, but I'm not going to specify which one. I can't see any point in hurting a junior mobster's feelings.

But let me tell you the story.

Mike, our Dalmatian, wasn't the most popular dog in town back in the '60s. Dr. Friedman down the street hated him because the dog often pooped on his porch.

Then there was the guy who owned two prize bantam roosters until Mike got into his yard and murdered them. My father drove all the way to New Hampshire to get some replacement roosters, but I don't think the rooster owner ever forgave Mike.

The pharmacist in town hated him, too. In summer, he used to prop his store door open and Mike considered that an invitation to go in and shoplift. The dog was partial to stealing paperbacks and suntan lotion.

Then the pharmacist would go down a few doors to my Uncle Alex's barber shop and complain. Uncle Alex was my mother's brother, and he was embarrassed about having a sister with such a hoodlum for a dog, so he'd call up our house and say come get your dog, the pharmacist is complaining.

Mike was a thief, a rogue and a chicken killer, and there was no shortage of folks who might have wanted to take out a contract on him.

The mobster's son did him in one June morning. He came speeding past our house and, when he saw Mike, he aimed right at him. Mike never knew what hit him.

I was devastated, as was my mother. My father felt bad, too, but I think my Uncle Alex was secretly relieved. He was tired of the pharmacist's complaints.

But we got over it, eventually, and as the years passed, a certain pride began to creep into our voices when we told the story about the mob hit on Mike. We always wondered who'd ordered the hit, and every now and again we'd run down the list of possibles.

Of course, in my heart, I figured it wasn't really a genuine hit. The junior mobster was also a junior driver, and not a very good one at that. More than likely, it was an accident.

But years later I was to find out otherwise.

In 1990, my oldest son Sean took a summer job as a doorman for one of those fancy apartment buildings on Park Avenue. He was a college student at the time, and he was lucky to get the job. Doormen make good money, and they don't exactly have to do any heavy lifting. Opening the limo door for the poodles on their way to the day spa was about as hard as it got.

So you can imagine that the doormen had some time on their hands, and they often got to talking. My son was always looking for a good story to tell in order to be one of the guys and not just considered the summer kid doorman. One day he decided to tell about the mob hit on his grandmother's dog in upstate Washingtonville.

I'm sure he figured the story was really just a crock, but it was a good bit of crock, nonetheless, and one worth repeating while doormanning.

Apparently the particular doorman my son was telling his story to had mob connections, and he got very intent while listening to the recitation of the facts.

Then he seemed to be struggling for a memory, my son tells me. Finally, he captured it because he said, "Well that must mean that your mother … nope, it must be your grandmother … your grandmother must be the sister of Alex the barber!"

Well, my boy's jaw just about dropped to the Park Avenue pavement. He hadn't said a word about Uncle Alex in the telling of the story.

"You mean to tell me you know Alex the barber?" my son asked the veteran doorman.

"Nope," the doorman said. "But I heard about that hit. I heard about Alex the barber's sister's dog getting taken out by the family. So that was your grandmother's dog! Small world, huh?"

Well, the story got passed along among all the Park Avenue doormen that summer. "Hey," one doorman would tell another, "this is the kid whose grandmother's dog got taken out by the family!" My son had gained stature.

As for me, I'd just like to tell the junior mobster that I forgive him. And I'd also like to thank him for providing my boy with a good story to tell on Park Avenue.

Mike c. 1959

'Mike was a thief, a rogue and a chicken killer,
and there was no shortage of folks
who might have wanted to take out
a contract on him.'

A Dog of Peculiar Habits

Cassidy came to be a member of our family as an ill-conceived reward to my two boys for not fighting. The day we got him, they had a fight over who would hold him on the way home.

Cassidy was one of a litter of eight, born under a trailer during a cold February. We did not pick him. He picked us. We had decided on his calm little sister and were on our way to the car when this white 6-week-old puppy-devil with floppy ears and a puzzled brow came trotting out of the nearby woods. He acted like he owned them. Unlike his brothers and sisters, who were sensibly curled in the lee of the trailer, this dog had been out exploring.

He stood beside the car door until we opened it. Then he climbed in.

We were chosen.

Cassidy is a mutt, but his dad was a yellow Lab, and that's who he took after. He's 10 months old now and he has yet to exhibit a modicum of common sense.

His body awareness, for example, is way below par. He's nearly 60 pounds, but he imagines himself the size of a toaster. He has caught his head between the cellar steps and wedged his body behind the toilet. When these things happen, he is genuinely baffled.

He isn't solid on our daily routine, either. No matter how patiently I explain what I'm up to, he still insists on going along for the ride when I move the car from the driveway to the garage. During the 20-foot trip, he sits ramrod straight in the back seat like the honored star of a ticker tape parade.

He's a bad dog, too. He thinks soapy water is for drinking, lawn mowers are for chasing and mascara is for eating.

He's personally responsible for damage to my kitchen linoleum, living room rug, drapes, window sills, dining room chairs, a couch, a sleeping bag and a pair of sneakers.

He gouged a deep hole in my son's room trying to make a housefly hold still, and now that the flies are all dead, he's got his eye on a spider.

And he's peculiar. He apparently likes heights because he often climbs trees, and I once caught him standing proud as a peacock in the middle of the dining room table. And he's devised a game of his

Cassidy with Brendan 1985

'*He apparently likes heights*
because he often climbs trees,
and I once caught him standing proud as a peacock
in the middle of the dining room table.'

own. He takes a running start down the wood floor of our long, central hallway. When he reaches midpoint, he squats on his haunches and goes into a slide that carries him clear through my bedroom. Generally, he saves himself before he crashes into my dresser, but not always.

He's also a slob. He spills water when he drinks. He routinely dumps the garbage. He wades through our neighborhood swamp, then climbs onto the beds. When he eats dinner, he lies down and straddles the dish with his gawky paws. He still has some puppy clumsiness in him, and now and then he knocks his dish over. When this happens, he leaps back in fright and stands staring at his mess as though he has no notion of who might have done this.

I just can't respect an animal like this. He belongs in a juvenile dog detention center. It's a mystery to me why I keep him.

"I really ought to get rid of that dog," I say to myself as I examine a freshly gnawed window sill. And then I hear my 10-year-old son Brendan laughing that deep, hearty laughter that can only come from the soul. The dog and the boy are in the bedroom, and the dog is dragging the boy out from under the covers by his underwear. This is Cassidy's boy, and it's time for him to wake up and play. The world is a marvelous place this morning, and he needs his boy to share it with him.

But I find myself picking up the garbage that he's scattered all over the lawn, and I say to myself, "I really ought to get rid of that dog."

And then Cassidy's 15-year-old boy Sean comes walking up the driveway. He's been away over night, and Cassidy leaps off the car roof in celebration of his arrival. The dog is beside himself with joy that this boy has returned from his travels, and he knocks him to the ground with his boundless exuberance. "Oh wow," says the boy. The dog keeps him company while he bandages his elbow, listening with rapt attention as the boy tells him about his evening.

But I discover a dining room chair that's chewed beyond repair, and I think, "I really ought to get rid of that dog."

And then he stretches awake from a nap on the new couch and comes over to drape himself across my lap for hugs. I am wearing a tattered bathrobe tied at the waist with old pantyhose. I have argyle socks on, and my hair is hanging in my face. No one but a dog would want a hug from me at this moment. Cassidy thinks I am lovely.

I suppose if I really want to respect an animal, I can always get a cat.

Test Your Dog's IQ

The trouble with Lassie was, she set an awfully high standard for dogs in the IQ department. All our dogs seem fairly inept by comparison.

Remember how smart Lassie was?

At least once an episode she'd approach a family member, usually Gramps, and have a conversation:

"Woof!" Lassie would say.

"What's that, Girl?" Gramps would say.

And Lassie would say, "Woof!"

"Oh!" Gramps would say. "You mean Timmy's foot is caught under a splintered floor board in the hayloft at the Owens farm, Girl? And there's an electric cable about to break and set the barn on fire?"

"Woof!" Lassie would say, and they'd both go off, and Lassie would save Timmy because she was a brave dog as well as a smart one.

The reason I bring this up here is because it might be our own fault that our dogs don't seem quite as bright as Lassie. It might be that we're not quite as bright as Gramps.

Most of time when your dog says "Woof!" you probably say, "Shut up, Stupid!" instead of listening, like Gramps did.

And you probably just assume that all the brains your dog has are stored in that tiny, little bump up on top of his head.

Well, that may be the case. But if you'd like to find out whether your dog has Lassie potential, it's a good time to give him…

The Dog IQ Test

1) Task Completion. Observe your dog when he scratches his ear. Does he start scratching himself and then forget what he's doing and sit there with his leg poised midair while he tries to figure out just what his leg's doing there?

Yes___ No___

2) Memory. Go outside. Come back inside. Does your dog knock you over in excitement because he's lost track of time and thinks you've been away on vacation and now you're finally back?

Yes___ No___

3) Deductive reasoning. Hold a tennis ball in your hand and pretend to throw it across the yard but really just hide it behind your back. Does your dog chase after it, even though you've played this trick on him a hundred other times?

Yes___ No___

Riley 2001

'Does he run out to the yard after his bath
and roll around in some carrion
or, if that's unavailable, some poop so that
he's more aesthetically pleasing?'

4) Planning Skills. Does you dog sometimes just stand up out of the blue and trot with great purpose into another room, like he's suddenly recalled he has some ironing to do, and then when he gets there he just kind of stares at air?

Yes___ No___

5) Bravery. During a lightening storm, does your dog try to cram himself behind the refrigerator?

Yes___ No___

6) Logic. Get on the bed with your dog. Put your leg underneath the covers (you can allow your dog to witness this maneuver) and then move it around a bit. Does your dog try to pounce on it and kill it?

Yes___ No___

7) Problem Solving. Offer your dog two things to eat at the same time.

Does your dog take both of them in his mouth and then carry them around for the afternoon because he thinks if he puts one down to eat the other one, he won't have it anymore?

Yes___ No___

8) Personal Hygiene. Give your dog a bath with some good-smelling dog shampoo, then spend quite a lot of time drying him off and brushing his hair.

Does he run out to the yard afterward and roll around in some carrion or, if that's unavailable, some poop so that he's more aesthetically pleasing?

Yes___ No___

9) Following Directions. Give your dog the following set of complicated directions:

"Get off the couch!"

Does he look at you reproachfully and then stretch out the full length of the couch to get more comfortable?

Yes___ No___

10) Common Sense. When you work out on your exercise bike, does your dog want to come along for the ride?

Yes___ No___

Give your dog one point for every "No" answer, and take away one point for every "Yes" answer.

If he scored in the Minus 10 range, he probably doesn't have much more brains than it takes to fill that little bump on top of his head.

If he scored in the Zero area, he's pretty much a Regular Dog, but don't make any appointments for screen tests.

If he scored on the Plus 10 side, congratulations! You're nearly as smart as Gramps!

Cassidy and Brendan 1984

*'We found his body
by the side of the highway
early in the morning.'*

A Case of Puppy Love

Cassidy died nearly three years ago, but I haven't been able to write about that until now.

He was an extremely busy dog the whole time I knew him. He always had something going on, kind of like a teenager with a hectic social life. Our big, old, black dog Molly thought he was a jerk right from the start. She insisted that he leave her in peace so she could slump in the sun like a dog is supposed to.

Although Molly wasn't charmed by him, Cassidy was a womanizer. He was a handsome Lab mix who never met a lady he didn't like, I guess. He had a special woman down the road, and we paid child support when their litter quit nursing and began eating store-bought food. It was only right.

But Molly treated him from the beginning like he was no more than a nodding acquaintance. Once in a while she'd bite him for good measure, but that was about all the attention he could get out of her. It wasn't until one morning when Cassidy was about 2 years old that Molly changed her mind about him. When she finally did, she came to adore him in a way that dogs usually reserve for humans.

It happened when Molly was sick. She had an abscess on her leg that I hadn't discovered until she was listless with a fever. The doctor said she was very, very sick. He sent her home with antibiotics, and she lay down in a corner of the dining room and stayed there. She didn't move all day and wouldn't go out at bedtime.

About six the next morning, Cassidy woke me up. He forced me out of bed, jumping back and forth from the bed to the floor until I could no longer ignore him. I followed him to the dining room, where he sat down next to Molly and looked at me expectantly.

Molly was stretched out on her side, panting shallowly. Her eyes were glassy, and her tongue was protruding. She was dying. I stood there helplessly. I didn't know what to do.

Cassidy did. He went to the water bowl in the kitchen and drank, then came back and dribbled water onto Molly's tongue. He did that twice before I caught on. I brought the bowl in, and he and I worked together getting water into her.

Then Cassidy wanted her moved. He stood behind her and began nudging her toward the door. He worked for several minutes until he irritated her into standing up. I opened the door so both dogs could go outside.

The movement did it. The abscess burst as she walked to her resting spot on the front lawn, and her fever broke soon after. Cassidy cleaned the wound for her.

He could do no wrong in Molly's estimation after that. She did anything he wanted, even if she didn't quite approve of it. He loved to go hunting with her, and she reluctantly went along even though she'd have to take to her bed for two days to recuperate after an all-nighter in the woods.

We never let both dogs out at the same time because we didn't want them hunting. They had to cross a highway to get to the woods. But Cassidy learned to open the screen door by jumping onto the handle, and Molly learned to follow close behind him before the door swung shut. Then they'd be gone.

Molly was with him the night he died. Generally, when they returned from hunting, Molly rested herself on the front porch while Cassidy came around to my bedroom window to wake me up. He'd hear my feet hit the floor and would run around to join Molly at the door to be let in.

Molly came home alone that night. She scratched at the door to let us know she was there. She came in and lay down in the corner of the dining room. She didn't sleep much; she just didn't move. She stayed there the rest of the night and all the next day.

We found his body by the side of the highway early in the morning. I believe the driver had stopped after the accident. Cassidy's body had been neatly placed by a road sign.

I don't know how long Molly sat with him before she came home.

Albany Seeks Top Dog

By Max, a dog

My name is Max. I am part Labrador retriever, part Democrat.

My woman said I could write her column today as I am very communicable and I have something of the uppermost impaction to report to you.

It's about our Official State Dog. New York doesn't have one.

But an Assemblyman from Long Island – which I am told is part of New York even though dogs there bark with a lungisland accent – wants to name the Labrador retriever the Official State Dog.

Think of it! Top dog in Albany! That's why I'm writing this, on account of I want to come out in favor of being the state dog.

The Assemblyman, whose name is John Behan, is a Republican, but I want to give the bill bi-species support.

I have had a lot of experience being a Labrador, which is because I am one, so on the behalf of all Labradors, I hereby say why this bill should be supported.

First, as you can probably tell, I am very intelligible. I speak clear and direct, which is more than can be said for most of the people in Albany. No one ever has to wonder where I stand on an issue. When I'm in favor of eating, for example, I say one word – usually "bark" – and the people know my feelings.

I don't talk doublebark.

Plus, I am very kind. I am so kind that one time I was visiting the little girl across the street and she had an ice cream cone. And I took turns with her licking the ice cream. We shared!

That's what government is all about. If you have something, then the government takes some of it! It's called sharing!

As you can see, I have a very sophistible understanding of how things work in the capital.

Also, I am very earnest and sincere. I earnestly and sincerely want what's best for all of us, which can be seen in my platform:

➤ Zero population growth. I did my part when I went to the hospitality and had the operation.

➤ A clean environment. By this I mean a scooper for every pooper.

➤ An end to the tax on dog food. What is this, a sin tax? A dog's gotta' eat, you know. It's humancentric to think that biscuits aren't one of life's necessaries.

There could be some fur flying over this. Some people might think that – what with New York City – maybe the Official State Dog should be a Rottweiler or a pit bull, who might bite your face off. Call me a cock-eared optimist, but I think with the Labrador, people might come to think of New York as a kinder, gentler state.

And I'm sure some uppity poodle out there might think the honor should belong to him. Think how humiliating that would be. He'd have to go to the hairdresser every time an official function came along. Jeez. This country's had enough of top dogs getting expensive hair cuts.

Some might even argue that the Official State Dog should be a mutt, such as my friend Molly (who is a Republican but who is very kind to me nevertheless). She doesn't even know who her father is! Are those the kind of morals we want to promote in state government?

(Not that I'm personally against mutts, of course. Like I said, I'm a Democrat. But it just wouldn't be befitting and dignant.)

Right now, Assemblyman Behan's bill needs a Senate sponsor. If you agree that the Labrador retriever should be Official State Dog, fill out the coupon attached to this article and mail it to:

Believers in Retrievers, c/o The Times Herald-Record, 40 Mulberry St., Middletown, NY 10940. (If you can't write, ask your woman or man to do it for you.) I'll mail this column along with your coupons to the top dogs in Albany.

Our barks will be heard!

Note: Despite lobbying efforts with the state legislature – Max sent hundreds of reader coupons up to Albany – no one in the Senate took up his fight.

Max eventually lost interest in the matter, mainly because he concluded that he preferred a good nap to running a state.

Come to think of it, he might have fit right in at the capital.

Scout 2001

'We can start here in the room of The Stinky Boy,
which is the room where The Stinky Boy sleeps
and keeps his socks.
This is my favorite room for smells because
The Stinky Boy has so MANY smells.'

amazing! – there are so many smells. I can smell something under here, under the hot box, which I know is hot because once I tried to smell it when the hot box door was open and The Not So Stinky Man said No, No Scout! Hot Scout! but not in time, no no no, and my nose got HOT so I put it in the cold toilet in the I'm Going To The Bathroom Leave Me Alone! Room.

But under the hot box are lots of smells I can smell. An old, old piece of spaghetti and a bacon smell, greasy bacon, and moldy ham, and a cracker and some of Scout's food and a faint faint very faint, carrot smell.

And the curtain, see on the curtain here, is a pizza smell where The Stinky Boy touched the curtain with his pizza hands and The Not So Stinky Woman yelled, Don't Don't Stinky Boy! Wash your greasy hands first!

And here, here, come here into the Watching Box room because in here there's another smell – very faint, very very faint, almost can't smell it any more – on the little rug near the fireplace. Not a Scout smell or a Max smell, no no no, it's an old dog smell, the smell of the Molly dog who used to live here before Scout came. A long time ago old dog smell. A good dog like Scout smell.

And the old dog smell is on the couch too, very faint, but the couch is the most amazing smelling place because it has such a lot of smells, so many many smells. Popcorn smells and an old penny smell and some snoring-sleep smell – a lot of snoring-sleep smell. And it has Scout's old bone smell, and the Max smell, and over here is The Other Stinky Boy's Girlfriend smell.

A totally excellent smelling couch.

And this is why The Not So Stinky Woman said to tell you she will not go to work next week no no no because she will stay home with Scout and Max and take away all the smells. And she wants the house to smell awful awful like pine and lemon and she wants to take away The Stinky Boy's socks in a garbage can!

She will be back in two weeks and Scout will be sad and bored by lemon smells but The Not So Stinky Woman will be happy yes yes she will and then she won't be ashamed to invite company over.

So then Scout will smell the company when they come. That will be so GREAT!

Scout Catches a Bug

It began as a peaceful enough evening. I was sitting on the bed, propped on the pillows, enjoying a mystery novel and a cup of tea.

Scout was lying next to me. Scout is an 8-month-old pup who I used to believe was a chocolate Lab, but she never grew. Now I figure she's just a little brown dog. Max, our other dog, was sleeping at the foot of the bed, snoring now and then and having that running dream dogs get once in a while, where their feet jerk all around.

So there we were, the three of us all comfortable and cozy, having a real Disney moment. Until Scout noticed the housefly.

The fly was sitting on my knee, rubbing its two little front legs together like it was preparing to have a meal. I expected to see it put on a bib at any moment. Scout stared at it for a while, kind of cocking her head this way and that, as though rearranging her brains might clarify the situation. She couldn't imagine what the thing was.

Finally she made up her mind to eat it, whatever it was, and she lunged at my knee. Naturally, the fly took off. Scout wasn't even close. But she was on Full Bug Alert now, and she watched that fly's progress as it traveled from curtain to ceiling to wall. At one point, it settled on Max's hiney, and she took another leap at it, but she was no match for that fly. Max ignored her and just kept on running in his sleep.

It was then that the fly made a critical mistake. It settled on the corner of my dresser, about three feet from the bed. Scout stared and cocked her head and stared some more. Then she inched her way to the edge of the bed. And that's when she lost control of what little sense she was born with.

She leaped off the bed, right onto the center of the dresser. She was so startled at finding herself in such an unseemly spot that she lost her balance and went crashing to the floor, pulling a bottle of liquid make-up with her. At the same time, her tail swung around and connected with the cup of tea on my night stand.

There she was, lying in a frightened heap with Shimmering Bronze make-up spattered all over her face and tea dripping off her ears. The fly was up on the ceiling, its little belly shaking with laughter.

The noise of the mishap awoke Max, of course, and he must have decided I was in some sort of danger. He leaped up, stiff-legged, and then lunged onto Scout's back, having determined that she was the culprit.

Scout's heart nearly stopped, I guess, and she let out a yelp as she scrambled under the bed, trailing her tail through the make-up so she could transfer the mess to my bedspread. Max lost interest in following her in favor of eating the make-up off the floor. Then he went into the kitchen and threw up. Max never did have a strong stomach.

Scout regained her composure under the bed and returned her attention to the fly, which now was settled on the cuff of my husband's navy blue corduroys. The pants were hanging on his clothes tree along with a good portion of the rest of his wardrobe.

Scout stalked the clothes tree. Finally, in a mighty rush, she leaped at the pants. With a loud clatter, the entire clothes tree came down on top of her. I thought maybe she'd managed to kill herself this time, it was so quiet under there. I carefully picked my way through the mess, wondering what I'd find underneath. But there she was, her face smeared with make-up, happily munching on the fly. She was proud as a peacock.

I had to wash the floors and launder the bedspread and my husband's wardrobe before I could get back to my book.

But, by God, there aren't any more flies in this house.

Bob Quinn

Scout with Beth 1991

'Scout stalked the clothes tree.
Finally, in a mighty rush,
she leaped at the pants.'

It's a Dog-Walk-Dog World

The whole thing happened because Max is so partial to the blue leash.

Max is our 5-year-old yellow Lab, and he generally acts as a dog should. He sleeps. He barks. He chews his butt.

Scout, the little brown dog, is about 18 months old now, and she rarely acts as a dog should. She flirts. She whimpers. She acts like a little girl.

Max doesn't entirely approve of her.

It's mainly a matter of principle, I think. He's quite a bit older and much bigger, and she's a sissy. Max believes he's in charge of making all the rules, which I guess he is. He gets the first biscuit at snack time. He gets to choose which chair to sleep in. And he gets to choose which leash he wants at walk time.

We have a brown leash and a blue leash, and the blue leash belongs to Max.

Every evening, as soon as we attach one end of the blue leash to his collar, he picks up the other end and carries it in his mouth during our walk. He never drops it.

The end result is, he looks like he's out walking himself, being responsible for making sure he doesn't allow himself to wander off. We just walk along beside him, holding Scout on the end of the brown leash.

Scout doesn't seem to object to this arrangement. She never cares to wear the blue leash herself. I don't think she even has an opinion about it, one way or another.

I wasn't paying attention the night I got the two leashes mixed up. I put the brown leash on Max. And I put the blue one on Scout.

I confess, I never noticed whether Max was making an issue of it, standing there by the front door.

My husband opened the door for them as he normally does. And the two dogs fled out to wait for us on the front lawn, as they normally do.

And when we joined them, Max grabbed up the end of the blue leash to walk himself, as he normally does.

And that's when I noticed my error. Max took off at a run with the blue leash in his mouth and Scout attached to the other end of

Scout, Max, Beth and her husband Bob 1991

'He looks like he's out walking himself,
being responsible for making sure he doesn't
allow himself to wander off.
We just walk along beside him,
holding Scout on the end of the brown leash.

it. Scout lurched after him.

She looked over shoulder at us in the darkness as they ran off. She seemed mystified by the turn of events.

We chased after them, and Max slowed them both down to a trot. They seemed to settle into a good pace together, the little one at the end of the leash keeping pace with the big one. Following at a distance, we began to think this might not be a bad thing. After all, if Max would walk Scout every night, it would save us a whole lot of trouble.

And things went smoothly, too, for at least 90 seconds. We began to congratulate ourselves as though we were responsible for this brilliant idea.

That's when Scout saw the Halloween ghost on one of our neighbor's lawns. It was one of those things with straw stuffed into some old clothing.

Scout's a sissy, like I said, so the straw man just about frightened her out of her fur, and she took off in the opposite direction.

Max, though, wanted to get a better look at that straw man. And so, with Scout's leash in his mouth, he headed right toward it. Scout lost the tug of war before it even began, and she found herself being yanked straight for the most frightening spectre she'd ever had to face in her young life.

She pulled back on the leash, but Max kept hauling. He inched along, with Scout in tow, closer and closer to the straw man. They were maybe three feet from it when I guess Max's mouth must have gotten tired from pulling her. Instead of dropping the leash, though, he swung around behind Scout to ease the tension.

Then he headed back for the ghost, making a complete circle of the leash around Scout. Then he circled her again.

By the time we caught up to them, those two dogs were the sorriest looking pair I've seen in a while.

There was Scout, rolling her eyes at that straw man looming over her, all trussed up in the blue leash like a calf waiting for the branding iron.

And there was Max, no slack in the leash left, with his head jammed beneath her tail. I guess he was determined to hang onto that blue leash no matter where it led him.

We got them untangled eventually – Max still wouldn't drop the blue leash so we had to walk him in circles around Scout to unwind him. Scout quit whimpering after awhile. We put the brown leash on her before we moved on.

As for Max, he got his sniff at the straw man, and he seemed satisfied. Wearing the blue leash and carrying its end in his mouth, he walked himself without incident the rest of the way home.

Scout Calls
for a Canine Congress

By Scout, the little brown dog

My name is Scout. I'm the little brown dog who belongs to the lady who usually writes this column, and I have something to say.

We dogs are in deep poop.

It's on account of Socks, that stupid cat who's moving into the White House. That cat is going to ruin our lives.

Already, 1993 has been declared the Year of the Cat.

Don't get me wrong. I'm part Democrat, just like Max. My mother was a Lab and my father – well, he was Affectionate.

But as a Democrat, Clinton is OK with me. It's just that Socks is working on a pro-cat agenda, and it's going to be our undoing.

Everybody knows cats are no good. They whine and sulk. They're nothing but cold-shouldered fuss-budgets.

Why, there's a cat in my own neighborhood who makes life a torture for me and Max. That cat marches up and down our driveway swishing her tail like she owns the place.

Max and I can't get to her although that doesn't prevent us from trying. We hurl our bodies against the door just to let her know we're in here, and we're working out how to turn that knob.

But that cat out there has an attitude, and she just goes on with her parading up and down the driveway as though we're no more intelligent than pine cones.

She's nothing but a trespassing law-breaker. When she finds out it's the Year of the Cat, she'll probably move right in and take over my couch and chair and bed and probably the toilet bowl, too, for good measure.

Cats already get too much attention. There are cute-cat cards, cartoons and calendars. Cute-cat stitchery, statues and stationery. Cute-cat balloons, books and buttons.

And things are going to get so much cuter in the Year of the Cat, I'm afraid I might just gag on a rawhide chewie.

We dogs missed the boat with that Millie. She seemed nice enough, but she just didn't have the juice to get anything done for us. In four years, we never once had a Year of the Dog.

So Max and I are calling for a Canine Congress – a grass-roots movement to put forth our own pro-dog agenda before that stupid cat completely takes over. We'll draft Ross PeRuff to be our spokesman.

We've already put together a partial list of proposals:

➤ We want research money earmarked for the development of some dognip. We fail to see why cats should have all the fun.

➤ We want equal rights in the greeting card business. Right now, cats outnumber dogs on greeting cards by at least five to one.

➤ We want phrases like "lazy as a dog" and "ugly as a dog" declared politically incorrect and insensitive.

➤ We want Social Security benefits for seeing-eye dogs, canine companions and sheep dogs.

➤ We want equality on the leash issue. Leash laws should apply to cats, too.

➤ And we want instructions on how to open the door so we can surprise the daylights out of that stupid cat out in the driveway.

If any other dogs have proposals you'd like added to our agenda, mail them to me. I'll send it on to the White House in January when Socks moves in.

Bob Quinn

Scout 1994

*'We dogs are in deep poop.
It's on account of Socks,
that stupid cat who's moving into the White House.
That cat is going to ruin our lives.'*

Brigette Olejniczak

Grandpup Jack meets Butch the cow 1999

'During the days of world exploration,
Magellan and other travelers brought dogs
along on the ships, where they would hang their heads
over the railing to 'catch sniffs.'

A Brief History of Dogs

Without getting too deep into the dangerous subject of religion, I wonder, just what purpose did God have for dogs when He or She invented them?

Well, I don't know.

But if we take a brief look at history, we can see some evidence that the purpose of dogs seems to have altered over the years, quite possibly so they could adapt to mankind's changing needs.

The Cave Dogs: It was during the Cave Dog days that canines first developed the most fundamental purpose of their existence – hanging around the hearth to eat any food that got spilled on the floor.

Because cave people didn't have brooms or Endust, this filled a valuable human need for cleanliness. Most breeds still have some sort of ancestral memory for this job, and they can often be found directly beneath our feet during food preparation.

Early Chinese Dogs: An adaptation of the Cave Dog's function was made in early Chinese culture, where a dog's job evolved from cleaning up leftover food to becoming the leftovers.

Fortunately, this use of the dog didn't spread too far, mainly because China was isolated and no one else heard of the idea.

Renaissance Dogs: These Shakespearean dogs were used mainly in a literary way, usually to provide "comic relief" during Shakespeare's many tragedies. Romeo and Juliet's families, for example, would occasionally take a break from their feud to laugh at the antics of Shakespeare's dog, Art.

The most memorable of these episodes is the balcony scene, in which Juliet takes time out from her sad musings to search for Art. Her line, "Wherefore Art thou?" is still famous.

The Explorer Dogs: During the days of world exploration, Magellan and other travelers brought dogs along on the ships, where they would hang their heads over the railing to "catch sniffs." They reliably alerted sailors to danger by "barking their heads off" whenever the ship passed a dog on another ship.

Many would continue to bark needlessly for the next 150 miles or until somebody threw them overboard.

The Pilgrim Dogs: This is when dogs first learned to "fetch." The Pilgrims, who were embarrassed by those stupid shoes with the buckles, taught their canine friends to fetch their slippers so they could take their shoes off as soon as they got home at night.

The Puritan Dogs: The main purpose of dogs during Puritan days was to watch the Puritans having sex to make sure they didn't enjoy it. Puritans were opposed to enjoying sex. In fact, they lived in the abiding fear that someone, somewhere might be having fun. It was against policy.

Anyone who owns a modern-day dog knows they still like to watch. This can sometimes put a damper on things.

Modern Day Dogs: Current dogs are used in many diverse ways. The purpose of some, such as mine, is to "sleep on the couch." It's the job of others to eat dead birds in the yard and then "throw up." Still others are responsible for "barking."

The Dog of the Future: Whatever direction mankind takes, it is likely the dog will continue to make an indispensable nuisance of himself.

The Dog of the Future will be catching sniffs on rocket ships, fetching their owners' gravity boots, and providing us all with comic relief like their ancestor, Art, did.

Max Goes to the Beach

By Max, a dog

This summer I went to the beach with my family plus Scout, the little brown dog.

While we were there, Scout and I spent most of our time being violators of the law.

We weren't supposed to go the beach. Right there on the lease for the house my parents rented, it said "NO PETS" in big words. Then it said "VIOLATORS will forfeit their lease."

VIOLATORS was spelled in capital letters on the lease, too, so it seemed like something I didn't want to be.

In general, I'm not inclined to be a capital-letter violator. I obey the rules of the road when I back-seat drive. And I make a point of curbing myself. Being a violator just goes against my grain.

But my mama said I'm not a pet, I'm a Labrador retriever, so as far as she was concerned, I wasn't violating anything. She expected that the people who owned the house wouldn't see the distinction, though, because Scout and I had to hide two times so strangers at the door didn't catch us violating.

I tell you, it violated my sense of dignity, crouching in the bath-room like a common criminal. I felt like a smoker, ostracized out of decent society as though I might cause second-hand cancer or some-thing.

The house wasn't the only problem. On the sign in front of the beach, it also said "NO PETS" in big red letters. "VIOLATORS will be prosecuted. $100 fine."

Well, I don't have $100 and my parents said I was definitely going to be arrested as a violator on the beach because it's hard to hide a pet out there in the open, even one who's a Labrador.

My mama said that unless I walked on two legs and wore a Speedo bathing suit, it was a cinch that someone was going to recog-nize my species situation. (Although, as far as I was concerned, some of the men on the beach wearing Speedos were definitely violators of good taste themselves. I'm no spring chicken, but even at my age I look better naked than a lot of those big-bellied, no-butted men in little bits of black fabric.)

So Scout and I only went to the beach at night, when it seemed all the dogs came out to violate. And it was there that my sensibilities

Max 1989

'When a wave comes in and knocks you silly,
don't sit down in the water again
because another wave is coming.'

got completely violated by a Law of Nature, which is mainly that when a wave comes in and knocks you silly, don't sit down in the water again because another wave is coming.

About the sixth time I got boomed in the head, my dad said I might want to notice that there was a predictable pattern going on here. But I guess I needed a little more Pavlov training because it took about a dozen head booms for me to realize there'd be a 13th one coming.

When the Law of Nature finally became clear to me, I shook the groggy out of my head and moved back on the sand a bit.

For her part, Scout, who is pretty much of a ninny anyway, was only willing to get her toes wet. Then she spent all her spare time digging in the sand for clamshells, which I felt was a profound waste of energy, as there were plenty of clamshells on top of the sand. But she seemed to be enjoying herself.

All in all, I'd say, we both had a good time being violators, and we never did get caught at it. Even so, next year, I think I'll stay home in my pool.

Either that, or I'll go to France on my vacation. I hear dogs are welcome everywhere in France, although Americans aren't too popular.

The end.

The Tale of the Pound Dog and the Purebred

Gus and Jack, my two grandpups, are both 10 months old now.

They're my boys' dogs, which makes me the closest thing to a grandmother that I'm likely to get for some time.

As I'm no fool, I know that puppy grandmothers aren't supposed to have favorites, and of course I don't. I definitely love them even-steven. So let me tell you about Gus, the costly purebred, and Jack, the genius pound dog, who are both equal in my book. Yesssirree.

My oldest boy, Sean and his girlfriend paid for Gus. (I confess to doing so myself, with most of my dogs.) They went to a breeder near Philadelphia, and they chose Gus from a litter of champion-line yellow Lab pups.

Melissa, Sean's girlfriend (now his wife), said Gus came to her when she called him from the litter. She interpreted this as a sign of intelligence.

As a high achiever, Sean quite naturally believed Gus would follow in his footsteps. He and Melissa bought eight or nine books – hard-cover books – on how to raise the perfect puppy. And they gave him the best start that life had to offer – his own cozy bed, 42 squeaky toys, chewies, and a special blankie.

(I admit to sending Gus a dog dolly and some biscuits by special delivery so he'd have them when he first arrived at his new home.)

His life was idyllic from the start – a play group at the park and a private puppy kindergarten attended by the best Philadelphia puppies. He was a perfect dog in the making with excellent parents.

Except that …

Well, let me introduce Jack before we get to the "except" part.

Jack belongs to my other boy, Brendan, and his girlfriend, Brigette (now his ex-girlfriend, which is a shame, not that anyone listens to me). They did not pay for Jack. Brendan went to the Middletown Humane Society, where he chose Jack from an abandoned litter of … well, mutts.

Jack looks like a shepherd, and he may well be one, but it is more likely that he is made of many things. He was somewhat imperfect at the start – a bit dandruffy, and he had bald spots on his tail, which the rest of the litter had been using as a chew toy.

Melissa Mullally

Grandpup Gus 1997

'His life was idyllic from the start –
a play group at the park
and a private puppy kindergarten
attended by the best Philadelphia puppies.'

Brigette Olejniczak

Grandpup Jack 1997

Brendan had no particular expectations of Jack. He lives in that sort of mellow New Paltz world, where a dog who goes to private school is considered something of a Nancy Boy. Jack would be home-schooled instead.

Jack selected a rather ratty blanket as his bed, and he seemed content with hand-me-down toys. As for dog-raising books, it turns out that if there were one in their apartment – which there isn't – Jack could read it himself.

Gus, God love him, chewed his books up, which is just as well because there's not one chapter in any of them on how to raise a hoodlum.

Right from the start, Gus displayed a cheerful indifference to the Rules of Puppy Society. He was held back in Sit and Stay Class because he's too "sociable" to sit and stay. Eventually, he was expelled. Sean was humiliated.

Gus is like a cartoon dog. He has eaten his way through Sean's desk. He has jumped headfirst into our rain barrel, nearly drowning himself. He has given himself a concussion by running into the side of a garage. He has engaged in thievery, stealing a whole roast beef off the kitchen counter. He's so chronically social that, when he visits, my own dogs go sit in the car to get some rest. In short, he's a really congenial simpleton.

Jack, on the other hand, asked Brendan for a list of the rules on his first day home. He was grateful to have a family after his earlier abandonment, and he probably didn't want to blow it.

He stands in their entryway if his paws are muddy until someone comes to wipe them. He sits. He stays. He rolls over. He retrieves the newspaper in the morning. He comforts the sick and visits with the homeless on the street. In short, he's a cheerful, brainy do-gooder.

Of course, I love them both equally. Absolutely no favorites. Even-steven all the way.

Any puppy grandmother would say so.

Grandpups Gus and Hank with Beth's daughter-in-law Melissa 2000

Chris Ramirez

Scout 2001

'Dogs are team players.
We get involved.
We're in the middle of everything,
from greeting visitors to your sex life.'

Cats Are No Good

By Scout, the little brown dog

I am Scout, the little brown dog who belongs to the lady who writes this column. And I want to say something I noticed about cats.

Cats are no good.

They are snobs. They make you feel like a jerk if you do something nice for them. They don't even care if you come home.

Dogs aren't like that. We show our appreciation by slobbering on you for even the smallest favor, such as if you go out of the room and then come back into the room. We're always excited to see you no matter how long you've been gone.

Cats are too soft. They aren't in good shape because they don't approve of exercise. They never take jogs with the people. If you throw a Frisbee at a cat, he won't even try to catch it.

Dogs are rugged. We're like cowboys. We can climb rocky terrain, and most of us can rope a steer. You can count on us to know what to do in a natural catastrophe. That's just how we are.

Cats are clean freaks. They spend all their time washing themselves and get very full of stress and disapproval over dirt. They need a support group to help them lighten up.

Dogs don't care. We'll go out and roll in a dead carcass and not bother tidying up for days. We're relaxed and comfortable with ourselves.

Cats are immoral. They're drug abusers. They take that catnip and get higher than a kite. Then they want more. They're little sociopaths.

Dogs have a clear sense of right and wrong. We don't use drugs. At the most, we have a beer once in a while, but that's it.

Cats are greedy yuppies. They eat cat food with names like Fancy Feast and they want it served in crystal goblets.

Dogs are down to earth. We eat food with names like Chuck Wagon and we don't even care if it's in a bowl. We'll eat right off of dirt.

Cats are fuss budgets. They don't want anything to disturb their perfect little lives. They get neurotic if someone moves the furniture. They sulk in the basement for days if their food isn't served at room temperature.

Dogs are calm and relaxed. We don't get upset if things aren't perfect. If a baby drools on us, we can deal with it. We don't get sullen when company comes.

Cats have weak stomachs. They get all clogged up with fur balls and throw up.

Dogs don't get digestion problems. We have bodies of iron. We can eat shoes and rocks, no problem.

Cats are selfish. They refuse to get involved in an issue and have no sense of justice. If a cat saw an intruder come into the house, he'd just turn his back and start cleaning himself. "None of my business," he'd say.

Dogs are team players. We get involved. We're in the middle of everything, from greeting visitors to your sex life. We make it a point to have everything in the house be our business, including that despicable cat.

Cats are lazy. They live little, low-maintenance lives so that, God forbid, they don't get dirty and have to start all over cleaning themselves again. They think it's too much trouble to have a relationship with someone because it might involve grime.

Dogs have a lot of energy. We interact in our relationships all the time. You got a dog, you got a ball, you got a game. We have the zip to get up 20 times an hour during a TV show to be let out, let in, let out, let in, let out, let in. That's just the way we are.

Cats were born old, but dogs are Peter Pan – always available for make-believe, no matter how old they get.

Dogs serve as a good example for children. They teach lessons such as loyalty, cheerfulness and the value of turning around three times before lying down.

No kid ever learned a thing from a cat.

Cats are no good.

The end.

When in Doubt, Ask Scout

By Scout, the little brown dog

I am Scout, the little brown dog who lives with the lady who usually writes this column.

She was going to write an advice column about dogs today, but then she said, "Scout! You do it. You're a dog. Who better to give dog advice?"

So I hereby present "Ask Scout," the only column in America about dogs, by a dog.

Dear Scout: They say that dog is man's best friend. Do you think this is true?

Dear Larry the Blade: How many of your friends have you neutered?

Dear Scout: My dog Buck, a well developed male, likes to be in the bedroom when my wife and I are … you know. What do you advise? I find it embarrassing, but my wife doesn't want to hurt Buck's feelings. Will this cause the dog to have psychological scarring?

Dear Dope: He's just a dog, for cryin' out loud. It's not like your boss wants to watch. Besides, what else does he have for entertainment? (See answer to question one.)

Dear Scout: My dog Lethargy does a lot of sitting around, doing pretty much nothing. What's going on inside his head?

Dear Freud: He's brooding over the fact that he's a dog. Do you have any idea what a bummer it is to be on the wrong side of a door without a thumb?

Dear Scout: Can you advise me as to what kind of dog I should get to guard the house?

Dear Coward: What's the matter with you? You want a dog to do your dirty work? Don't you have the guts to bite people yourself?

Dear Scout: My two dogs are constantly bickering over their toys and bones. How do I get them to share?

Dear Pollyanna: Sharing is highly over-rated. What's the point in giving someone else your stuff? What's the point in letting someone else keep his own stuff? Dogs don't share, barter, trade, buy, sell or otherwise engage in the economy. Dogs steal.

Dear Scout: I'm considering getting a cat but am unsure whether my dog will welcome one into our home. What do you advise?

Dear Judas: Cats are no good.

Dear Scout: Every once in a while, just for my own amusement, I like to mess with my dog's head. Are there any head games you'd recommend?

Dear Sadist: Two words. Peanut butter.

Dear Scout: What's the politically correct way of saying "mutt"?

Dear Miss Manners: You can say "pedigree-challenged" or "the results of random sex in the neighborhood."

Dear Scout: Can you recommend any games that I might play with my dog?

Dear Simple-minded: One good game is called Go Outside and Then Come Back Inside. Your dog will enjoy standing with his nose in the crack of the door while awaiting your return.

Dear Scout: When I walk my dog and he wants to relieve himself, is there some sort of etiquette for whether or not I should look?

Dear Blooming Idiot: Your dog is naked. He chews at his private parts in the center of the road. He glares at his own butt when he passes gas. Modesty isn't an issue.

Dear Scout: My dog seems to enjoy it when I read to him. Can you recommend any literature appropriate for him?

Dear Person in Need of Some Grandchildren: You could start with Shakespeare's Dog Stories. There's the humorous story of Spot, about a dog's antics as Lady Macbeth tries to house train him. Much of the dialogue consists of "Out, out, damned Spot!"

And there's the story of Toby, the dog who languishes in a shelter cage while Hamlet agonizes in his famous soliloquy about whether or not to choose him: "Toby or not Toby? That is the question."

Dear Scout: My dog is inordinately fascinated by my computer monitor. Do you suppose he can read?

Dear Dot.com Brain: Of course your dog can't read. He's waiting for you to open Windows so he can stick his head out.

Scout and Bob 2002

Chris Ramirez

'Dear Scout: My dog Buck, a well developed male,
likes to be in the bedroom when my wife and I are …
you know. What do you advise?
I find it embarrassing,
but my wife doesn't want to hurt Buck's feelings.'

Tom 2004

*'Every yard would be stocked
with an automated Frisbee thrower.'*

New Rules When Dogs Rule

From a dog's point of view, the world is fraught with inconvenience.

Not only do sun spots move when least expected, but the place is simply teeming with small children who like to put tails in their mouths.

Seems to me that if dogs were in charge, there'd be a few changes around here. Be my guess that if dogs had their way:

➤ Beds would be round to make it easier to turn around in circles before lying down.

➤ Dog food ads in magazines would come with scratch 'n sniffs.

➤ Drooling would be a highly respectable standard of behavior.

➤ All cars would come equipped with a sniffolator – a nose-operated opening for dogs to stick their heads out and get some sniffs any time they feel like it.

➤ Children would be forbidden from taking up musical instruments.

➤ Humans would have to kick the boss when they're mad at the dog.

➤ All doors would close slowly enough for dogs to get out with their tails still intact.

➤ Humans would be required to get badtemper shots each spring.

➤ Television would be three-dimensional so dogs could figure out just what it is the humans are looking at. "Lassie" would be available in sense-around.

➤ The mail carrier would have to quit touching people's houses.

➤ "I brake for animals" would be a law instead of a bumper sticker.

➤ There would be a fire hydrant in every yard.

➤ Dog food would come in flavor variety packs.

➤ Cats would have to work. No more of this lying around while dogs hold down all the jobs. There would be retriever cats, seeing-eye cats, sheep cats, guard cats and cop cats to help out with catnip busts.

➤ There would be a bed in every sun spot.

➤ Humans would have to turn over all the pizza crusts to the dogs.

➤ Sniffing crotches would be an acceptable greeting.

➤ An after-bath spray that smells like dead meat would be developed.

➤ Babies would be kept in the attic until they develop enough sense not to poke a dog in the eye.

➤ Every yard would be stocked with an automated Frisbee thrower.

➤ Fireworks would be quiet.

➤ Humans would be required to fetch their own damn sticks.

A Germanshepherddog of Uncommon Distinction

There's a new noise in our house now. It sounds like, "Click click click click click click Aarrgggggghh!"

The "Click click click click click click" part is our dog Riley's nails hitting the floor as he searches the house for me, which happens whenever it occurs to him that I might have moved away since he last saw me 10 minutes ago.

The "Aarrgggggghh!" part is how I express pain. When he locates me, it's not enough for him to simply say, "Hey ma'am (he calls me ma'am), glad to see you haven't taken off with the beef jerkies." Instead, in his enormous enthusiasm at discovering that both I and the jerkies are still on the premises, he hurls himself at me and smacks me in the head. I've got brain damage from so much affection.

This kind of greeting would be less of a headache if Riley weren't a 100-pound German shepherd dog. That's how dog experts say it, by the way – "German shepherd dog" – all three words, as though someone might otherwise confuse him with a "German shepherd llama."

Actually, we're not certain he's a genuine Germanshepherddog because we got him from a local shelter, where he'd been unceremoniously dropped off in the middle of the night at the age of about 10 weeks. An accounting of his lineage wasn't included in the package – no piece of paper saying we can trace his royal ancestry back to the 15th-century champion, Sir Black Forest Cake the Fifth or something equally impressive.

But the same dog experts who say "Germanshepherddog" also claim he sure looks like a genuine, purebred Germanshepherdog, mainly on account of ears the height of a skyscraper. Also, his general slathering attitude toward our guests gives him a shepherd-like guard dog demeanor. We didn't have that many friends to begin with, and now Riley's used them all up.

On the other hand, some horse experts claim that he looks like a genuine, purebred Clydesdale, mainly on account of the fact that his feet are the size of dinner plates.

Riley 1998

*'We didn't have that many friends to start with,
and now Riley's used them all up.'*

We came to own this lifestyle-altering dog after Max, our really
relaxed yellow Lab, died some time ago. (Max, some of you may
recall, once lobbied in Albany to have the Labrador retriever named
the official state dog, but his efforts went largely unrewarded because
our lawmakers were too busy thinking about maybe passing another
late budget.)

Anyhow, it wasn't exactly our decision to adopt him. Our boys,
who are actually men now, have concluded that my husband and I
have become old people. They feel we've reached the age whereby we
can't be entirely trusted to handle our own affairs although I'm happy

to report we're not yet wandering around the house naked trying to recall where we keep the food.

But the boys advised us to get another dog right away after Max died, and they involved themselves in the process.

Our youngest boy found Riley at the shelter, and he said we should "just come and look at this adorable, little guy." He tricked us, of course, although you'd think we'd know by now that all dogs are both adorable and small when they're babies – even those who shortly grow to the size of a Volkswagon.

Scout, our little brown dog – who, at the age of 9 is actually our little gray dog now – thought we'd lost our minds when she got a look at Riley.

"Are you completely nuts?" she said in that lecturing voice of hers. "I just finally got to be the main dog around here, and now you've gone and gotten an EXTRA dog?! And look at him! He looks like the Sears Tower with those ears."

Despite her poor attitude toward him, Scout is the only one who Riley treats tenderly. In fact, he nearly knocked me out in the middle of the night Friday expressing his concern for her. She was feeling poorly – making those noises a dog makes just before puking up a tennis ball –and this prompted Riley to wake me up to minister to her.

I, of course, didn't know what was on his mind. All I knew was that, when I opened my eyes in the dark, he had his dinner-plate feet planted on either side of my head and his nose was in my eye. Then he head-butted me.

"What! What!" I shouted. I was deeply confused. "Are you Cujo or something!?" I tried to extricate myself from between his legs and reach for my Louisville Slugger at the same time. "Did you get a case of rabies after I fell asleep or something?!"

He drew my attention to Scout by butting my head in her general direction. Then, satisfied that I was on the job, he sat down to study the tossed-up tennis ball mess she'd made as though it were a remarkably interesting ancient language.

I've taken to wearing my boy's old football helmet around the house. Maybe I'll wear it to bed, too. It just seems easier than having to explain at the e.r. how I keep getting these concussions.

The Life of Riley

Our German shepherd dog, Riley, is self-entertaining.

He has to be because the rest of us are boring. My husband and I don't play Frisbee, and Scout, our elderly little brown dog, mainly sleeps. So Riley has invented some primitive games to keep himself amused. Here are some of them, along with the rules of play.

Put the Chewie. This game commences when I give Riley a chewie. Instead of chewing the chewie, he scampers around the house to find a place to put it.

(OK, he doesn't actually scamper. At 100 pounds, scamper doesn't really apply. I'd say lumber is more like it.)

Anyway, Riley Puts the Chewie someplace. Sometimes between the couch and cushion, sometimes standing upright against a wall, sometimes into the toilet.

Check on the Chewie. This game lasts for the rest of the day. Riley sometimes remembers that he Put the Chewie and, when he does, he returns to see if anyone messed with it. Sometimes Scout messes with it just to screw with his head.

Toss the Bone. This game involves a soup bone and hard floor. The rules are: Put the bone in your mouth, toss it in the air, let it drop onto the floor. Do it over and over and over and over or until such time that someone Takes the Bone.

Poke the Screen. In this fast-paced event, involving both indoor and outdoor fun, Riley responds to some outside stimulus, such as a child on a bike.

Then he races from window to window, yelling and poking his nails through the screens. The child responds by pedaling really fast.

Bark at a Bug. This game involves complex inter-species communication. The bug begins the play by entering the house after a session of Poke the Screen. Riley takes over the action when he spies the bug and barks and barks and barks and barks and barks.

The bug dies from sheer boredom.

Expose the Genitals. This "kids will be kids" activity commences when a visitor approaches the door.

Riley 2002

'*Riley responds by jumping*
onto the dining room window next to the door
and stretching himself to his full height,
thereby exposing himself to our company.'

Riley responds by jumping onto the dining room window next to the door and stretching himself to his full height, thereby exposing himself to our company. Company responds by leaving. End game.

Hide in the Tub. This isn't a game so much as evidence that Riley is as neurotic as Woody Allen. He Hides in the Tub whenever anything falls from the sky. Right now, it's falling leaves that have him upset.

He also Hides in the Tub when it rains, snows and – on a just-in-case basis – whenever an airplane flies overhead.

Sometimes, I Put the Chewie in there with him to keep him entertained.

Would the Dog Eat the Baby?
(The Saga of Riley and Bella)

The dog was a puzzle
When Bella was born.
Would the dog eat the baby?
I really was torn.

The baby belonged to
My very good friends.
Would the dog eat the baby?
I said, it depends.

Just what is a baby?
The dog didn't know.
Is it something to eat?
He might decide so.

Will he think it's a cat?
Will he think it's a skunk?
Will he grab at her arm
And take a big chunk?

Will he think it's a rag
That we keep in the trunk?
Will he think it's a chewie?
If so, then we're sunk.

The dog is called Riley,
A hundred-pound shepherd.
He scares off the man
Who delivers The Record.

He leaps at the window
Warning all who arrive.
This is MY house, he says.
Do you want to survive?

So the dog was a worry
When Bella was new.

Would the dog eat the baby?
It just couldn't be true!

Her parents came over,
The baby all swaddled.
I reassured Riley,
Just hugged him and coddled.

I love you, big Riley,
I love Bella, too.
So come here and meet her.
Yes, come hear her coo!

The dog was suspicious,
His ears pricked up high.
He pranced back a pace,
Then turned tail to fly.

He ran to the basement,
To one of his lairs.
I found him aquiver
Hid under the stairs.

Just what is a baby?
The dog didn't know.
Is it something to eat?
He might decide so.

For an hour or two
He sneaked up and down.
He sniffed at her head
Then leapt off the ground!

A coward, 'tis true,
But the jury was out.
Would the dog eat the baby?
Would there always be doubt?

Just then little Bella
Let loose with a bubble.
A pants bubble that is
(A sure sign of trouble).

But the dog was enchanted
By that sound from the baby,
He forgot to be nervous,
His tail started waving!

Her mother undressed her,
Her diaper – so tiny!
Riley edged even closer.
The dog sniffed her hiney.

Oh! said the dog to
Himself (I'm assumin').
I know what that smell is,
This baby is human!

I want her! he thought,
This baby is mine!
He stuck out his tongue
And he licked her behind.

And so it was clear that
A friendship was started.
The dog and his baby
Would soon be unparted.

When she tossed him a ball
Or wanted to hide,
The dog was right there
To play by her side.

If the dog got too rowdy,
She waved her small fist.
As soon as she did this,
The dog, he'd just sit.

But still we watched closely
When Riley was with her.

Would the dog eat the baby?
We couldn't be sure.

And then came the evening
That Riley was tested.
I had failed to watch closely,
My vigilance rested.

The grown-ups were gab-
bing
While the dog and his pal
Romped in the living room.
Then … we all heard a
growl.

My heart turned to ice
At that sound from his
chest.
I thought I would have me
A cardiac arrest.

We raced to the living room
To see what was up.
Did the dog eat the baby?
Would he do this, my pup?

But the scene that we found
When we ran to that room
Made me realize right off
That I'd judged him too
soon.

At the fireplace hearth
The baby was climbing.
Bright flames – oh so pretty!
The sparks, they were flying.

Our Riley was warning,
Come rescue my hon!
I'd do it myself
But I don't have a thumb!

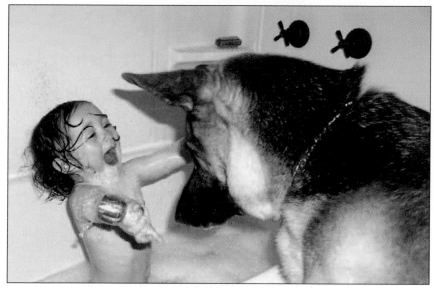

Riley and "his" baby, Bella Ramirez 2003

'And then came the evening
That Riley was tested.
I had failed to watch closely,
My vigilance rested.'

And so we retrieved her –
She never stopped giggling.
The dog licked her gently –
She never stopped wiggling.

We've stopped all our worry,
There's no longer fear.
Will the dog eat the baby?
The answer is clear.

Just what is a baby?
Our Riley, he knows.
She's someone to cherish
And guard as she grows.

Regal Riley,
the Wild-Eyed Watchdog

As a German shepherd dog of noble stature and regal bearing, Riley is the epitome of tireless guardianship.

His stamped look of quality – that cleanly chiseled head and distinctly masculine build – is the culmination of fine breeding. His commanding presence fills me with pride, and I find myself feeling pity for those saddled with lesser dogs.

And then it thunders. There is, in fact, a distant rumble in the sky as I write.

I would like to think that Riley is sitting in my bedroom closet because he feels duty-bound to protect my clothes from the storm.

I am, in fact, predisposed to believe that the preternaturally keen intuition of my fearless companion informs him that this closet is most vulnerable to the coming storm's wrath.

Riley the Bold has hurled himself into the path of danger – crushing my hiking boots, drooling on my open-toed sandals and shedding on my black dress – because he knows far better than I that this particular spot needs his full protection. He is the Praetorian Guard of my jeans.

I am certain Riley is highly intelligent. He holds his head erect, his ears tilted well forward. His eyes are shining and alert, his expression composed. Usually, anyhow.

I am the one who's the fool for failing to recognize, as he does, that the world is coming to an end.

The thunder rolls slightly closer and I remain oblivious to the danger, carrying on the mundane chores of the simple-minded. I go to the cellar to bring up the laundry.

In his industrious guardianship, Riley emerges from the closet to follow and protect me. He stays close. So close, in fact, that he steps on my feet as I try to negotiate my way down the cellar steps.

How my majestic defender must adore me! True, I nearly trip over my courageous escort and break my neck, but how faithfully he stays glued to my thigh!

I open the dryer door and reach in. Just then – Boom! – a thunderclap crashes directly overhead! All right. It was a low rumble in the distance, but still!

*'My valiant chaperon manages,
somehow, to maintain a certain degree
of wild-eyed poise as he extends his forelegs
and scrambles into the dryer.'*

My valiant chaperon manages, somehow, to maintain a certain degree of wild-eyed poise as he extends his forelegs and scrambles into the dryer.

How agile he is! And how dignified! He is a large, woolly caterpillar curled up on what had been, only a moment ago, my clean sheets. He has already shed the equivalent of 10 small dogs on them.

My stately champion peers out at me from beneath a paw, his glazed expression communicating what I am certain is a gallant invitation to join him in this safe haven.

If only there were room!

The storm keeps raging – well, some light rain drips, anyhow – as I retreat up the steps, leaving my proud sentinel in the dryer to keep guard over the dirty sheets.

Upstairs, Scout, my little brown dog, is asleep on the couch, indifferent to Doomsday. Alas, poor Scout. Such a simple, placid soul. Clearly, she lacks the finely honed intelligence needed to know she, too, should be hiding in the dryer.

I sit down beside her and we watch TV. At long last, Riley untangles his well-muscled limbs and climbs out of the dryer. Then – my champion! – he comes upstairs to signal that the crisis has passed. He takes a richly deserved swig from the toilet.

With gratitude in my heart, I return to the cellar to rewash the sheets.

My gallant knight-errant has, once again, seen us safely through a spring drizzle.

Riley 2000

Dominick Fiorille

Cassidy with Sean 1984

Primer on Dog Mythology

Everyone knows dogs worship people. That's why we like them.

"Buck just worships the ground I walk on," we say, and then we kind of puff up with feelings of importance.

But what most people don't know is that dogs have a very complicated and sophisticated set of myths that help guide them in their worship of us. Their mythology contains tales of the many major and minor gods that rule their world.

For those of you unfamiliar with dog religion, the following Primer on Dog Mythology should help.

Major gods and goddesses

The head man god is Prosperous, also known as Billpayer and God of the Remote Control. He drives off in his chariot Volvo each day after the sun rises and disappears into the Great Unknown until the sun completes its journey across the sky.

On special feast days, called Weekends, Prosperous allows dog to ride in Volvo, where dog engages in the ritual Sacrifice of the Spittle, in which he hangs his tongue in the wind and slobbers into the sky.

Haira, wife of Prosperous and Goddess of Dirt, is the head woman goddess. Known for her great patience with dog and the other gods and goddesses, Haira controls the fearsome Air Sucker, a machine that gathers dirt and dog hair. She is also the Keeper of the Toilet Bowl Shrine for dog.

Odiferous, the baby goddess, is daughter to Prosperous and Haira. Commonly known as the Goddess of Pollution, tiny Odiferous is the true ruler of the household. She often raises a stink to summon the attention of Prosperous and Haira. This small goddess can be among the most dangerous to dog, for she often pulls dog's tail. If dog shows anger with Odiferous, he incurs the wrath of Prosperous and Haira and can be cast out of the household.

Frisbee, the boy god, is son to Prosperous and Haira and the older, resentful brother to Odiferous. Like dog, Frisbee often sulks at the presence of Odiferous. The two console themselves by playing with the discus, which Frisbee throws into the sun for dog to catch.

Acne, the two-headed adolescent god, is son to Prosperous and Haira and brother to Odiferous and Frisbee. Also known as the Mood God, he can change the atmosphere from sunny to stormy

*'Humpicus, the God of Human Thighs,
is among dog's favorite gods.
The appearance of Humpicus
at the home of Prosperous and Haira
marks the beginning of the Festival of the Sniffs.'*

without any warning. Acne worships at the temple of the female goddess Aphrotelephonee, who holds the power to rip Acne's heart in two.

Chaos, the adolescent goddess, is daughter to Prosperous and Haira and sister to Odiferous, Frisbee and Acne. Known also by the names Queen of the Prom and Goddess of Melodrama, the household of the deities is often in an uproar when Chaos is present. Chaos is the most difficult of the gods for dog to understand. As she performs the Ritual of Dressing, for example, she can be heard wailing, "I don't have anything to wear."

Minor gods and goddesses

Biticus is the fleet-footed God of the Postal Service. According to legend, Biticus is doomed to travel the neighborhood by foot carrying a bag of paper. Dog believes Biticus to be an enemy to his household deities and dutifully performs the Ritual of Barking whenever he arrives.

Tortuous, a powerful healer god, performs rituals to ward off evil. Tortuous cures sickness by shining a light into dog's eye, by putting a flat stick into dog's mouth, and sometimes by putting a long, silver needle into dog's leg. He has great power, but dog fears his instruments of magic.

Humpicus, the God of Human Thighs, is among dog's favorite gods. The appearance of Humpicus at the home of Prosperous and Haira marks the beginning of the Festival of the Sniffs.

Cassidy with Brendan 1985

Scout 1994

Bush's Dogs Hold Key to Pretzel Caper

I fell down in my living room once.

Not on account of eating a pretzel like the president did last weekend. Just on account of being a klutz.

But here's the thing. Unlike Barney and Spot Bush, who mysteriously failed to take an interest when their master landed on the floor, my two dogs investigated with enormous canine concern. In fact, I couldn't get off the floor without first submitting to a full-body examination.

Scout and Riley checked my ears, nose and throat. They tested for broken bones. And for good measure – and because, after all, they're dogs – they checked on my butt while they were at it.

Fortunately, I came away from the incident with fewer bruises than the president did. On the other hand, I needed to boil myself to get rid of all the dog slobber.

Anyone with a dog knows that lying on the floor – either on purpose or by fainting from a pretzel – is going to elicit prompt dog involvement.

The floor is theirs. If you're lying on it, they figure it could be a game or you could be dead. Either way, they don't ignore you. One second you're looking at the ceiling, and the next you're looking at a furrowed, hairy brow.

And, in my case, I'm also looking at a big mouth with a ball in it. Riley, our shepherd, shows up for all events with a ball on the off-chance that even a dead person might want to play fetch.

My question is, what's up with Barney and Spot? Bush said his dogs were in the exact same position before he fainted as when he woke up. They just sat there!

After hearing this, a lot of Americans called the White House to question the moral turpitude of Barney and Spot. Bush spokesman Ari Fleischer defended the dogs, assuring the press that they "showed a lot of concern on their faces."

I never saw a concerned dog sit still. When dogs are concerned, they act like Gerald McBoing-Boing. They stick their noses directly into the matter of concern.

I believe this is a White House cover-up. Based on Barney's and

*'Fortunately, I came away from the incident
with fewer bruises than the president did.
On the other hand,
I needed to boil myself
to get rid of all the dog slobber.'*

Spot's behavior, I think we can conclude that one of the following is the real truth of the matter:

➤ This is no isolated event. Bush is always fainting from eating pretzels because he doesn't chew 30 times before swallowing. He's in a constant pretzel swoon.

➤ Barney and Spot hate Bush and agreed beforehand not to help should he ever faint.

➤ Bush didn't really faint. Someone in the White House caused the bruises by decking him for eating all the pretzels.

We need a congressional hearing to get to the bottom of this. Scout has agreed to depose Barney and Spot.

Riley will bring the ball.

Cassidy 1984

Scout and Riley 2003

Sleeping Class Dogs a Breed of Their Own

I was sitting like a lump on my couch when the Westminster dog show came on.

So was Riley, our German shepherd dog. He was curled up next to me, occasionally raising one eyebrow to watch as some well-muscled Sporting Class dog pranced across the screen. Riley maintained a perfectly executed position of utter sloth.

Scout, our little brown dog, slept soundly on her feather bed. If she took any notice of the athletic Working Class dogs, she managed to convey a beautifully composed expression of total indifference.

As I watched the proud champions on television, I felt a bit like I do when Olympic gymnasts are on – as though I should rise from the couch and do a split in an ill-conceived effort to prove I'm still flexible.

In this case, though, I wanted to proudly raise Riley's tail straight up in the air and adjust his hind legs into the same regal pose the champion bloodhound was holding. I wanted to show off his noble bearing.

Scout was off the hook, not because she's not the best little brown dog ever, which she is, but because there is no Little Brown Dog category. The AKC has never set standards for such a breedless little breed.

A little brown dog doesn't require balance in the forequarter, has no need for a moderately arched forehead, and doesn't have to be nimble of foot, incorruptible of character and flexible of loin. A little brown dog can be anything she wants.

But Riley – he's a breed. A Herding Class dog. There are standards for dogs like Riley. And so I went to the cellarway and got out the yardstick. I was going to determine just how my Riley would stack up.

I'd have to do it without waking him, though. He had turned in for the night.

I began by running my hands over his withers, just as the judges were doing. At least, I think I was feeling his withers, although I'm not certain what a wither is. Perhaps I was feeling his knees, instead.

'I began by running my hands over his withers,
just as the judges were doing.
At least, I think I was feeling his withers,
although I'm not certain what a wither is.
Perhaps I was feeling his knees, instead.'

Whatever I was feeling, they seemed to "have substance without cloddiness," which is important. He'd probably have even more substance if he were awake and standing up, but I did my best.

I straightened him out the full length of the couch before I began measuring. He seemed to be about 27 inches tall at the shoulder when my husband held his legs out stiff. Overall length was about 31 inches, give or take. Fabulous.

I checked his lips. They had a nice, flexible quiver as he snored. I also noted that his front legs would be directly under his body if he were standing up – another good sign. Coat, good. He's an excellent shedder. Head, perpendicular to the floor when he's awake and upright. Eyes, lovely when open.

He's a fine physical specimen. Unfortunately, he would make an ass of himself at a dog show. Instead of trotting in the ring, he'd find a cushion to lie on and stick his legs in the air in open invitation for a rub. He'd do fine at a Belly Rub Invitational, but he'd merely drool on the freshly blown-dry Welsh corgis at such a dog show as this.

I put away the yardstick and took a hard, critical look at my slothful dogs, ashamed of their lower-class bearing. But as I settled back onto the couch and curled up with my snoring German shepherd dog, Sleeping Class, it occurred to me:

Scout and Riley do what dogs do best. They've adopted our lifestyle. They don't care about splits during the Olympics or firm withers during Westminster. They've entered our lives of perfectly indolent comfort, happily and without judgment.

My dogs are perfect. Scout, Best of Non-Breed. Riley, Best of Show-Watchers.

Grandpup Gus with Beth's grandson Sam 2004

Max 1988

Grandpup Jack with two statues 2005

Riley 2003

Tom 2003

Huckleberry Quinn 2003

Of the People, by the People, for the Dog

When our family government was established years ago, I was named both minister of finance and minister of the interior.

My husband is minister of arts and leisure as well as minister of the environment. Riley, our German shepherd dog, is our current defense minister.

Scout, our aging little brown dog, is not minister of anything. It is for her, as far as she is concerned, that the family government exists.

As minister of the interior, it is my job to launder the cover of her goose down dog bed once a week and to keep the toilet bowl clean for her drinking pleasure.

Part of my portfolio as minister of finance is to budget a disproportionate amount of the family income each payday to the purchase her chewies, squeaky babies and the occasional soup bone.

My husband's tasks in the role of minister of the environment include poop patrol in the yard and the cultivation of flower gardens for Scout to lie in. He also maintains the area beneath the forsythia, as it is Scout's preferred cool spot on a hot day.

My husband's primary duty as minister of arts and leisure is ball-throwing. Rubber balls in summer and snowballs in winter. These last require careful aim so Scout can catch them midair. Should they fall short, she grows frantic as she digs in the snow to locate … more snow. It is a losing proposition.

The minister of arts and leisure is also responsible for signaling the time to commence Scout's evening outing. This is largely a matter of saying to me, "Are you ready to go for a w-a-l-k?" This last word is spelled out rather than spoken in order to avoid the inevitable pre-walk frenzy.

Alas, this clever ruse lost its purpose years ago, when both dogs figured out that when the minister of arts and leisure says "w-a-l-k," he means "walk." The minister has tried switching to "s-t-r-o-l-l," but that has failed utterly. They know.

In any case, there is always a great deal of bouncing and bounding and barking while the minister and I put on our shoes, attach the leashes and arrange ourselves at the front door for the launch to departure.

*'When our family government was formed,
we deluded ourselves that we were a democracy.
Alas, this was but a Jeffersonian dream.
We are, instead, a monarchy. Hail to Queen Scout.'*

My husband's job on the "arts" end of this particular ministry is the least taxing of his workload, as it is limited to turning on the TV in the evening. Thus, Scout can settle on the couch beside him for the between-show rubs that are her due.

As defense minister, Riley's portfolio is a reasonably full-time affair. There is an enormous number of threats to our family government, ranging from squirrels to Jehovah Witnesses, and he's responsible for patrolling the perimeter of da fence (hence his title) and protecting our headquarters.

Scout, in her dotage, has turned over all such responsibility to Riley. At best, when he barks a warning, she raises her head from her goose down bed to judge whether or not the threat is genuine. The UPS man falls into the high-alert category, a kind of Code Red for our family's citizens.

It is only on these occasions that Scout offers to serve as backup. As Riley mans the ramparts at the dining room window, Scout hruffs a time or two from a prone position. Satisfied that she has done her part, she returns to the business of napping.

When our family government was formed, we deluded ourselves that we were a democracy. Alas, this was but a Jeffersonian dream. We are, instead, a monarchy.

Hail to Queen Scout.

Grandpups Gus and Little Mac 2004

Grandpup Jack 2003

Bargaining with Time for the Little Brown Dog

Scout chased a squirrel this morning.

This would be unremarkable but for the fact that, a few weeks ago, we had arrived at the point where my husband was carrying her outside to relieve herself.

Arthritis had frozen her hips. The cold winds of January, seeping in through the cracks, had stiffened her bones. No amount of featherbeds or painkillers helped her.

Our little brown dog is 12 now. Aside from her bad hips and white muzzle, though, she is still our cheerful pup. Arthritis has never slowed the wag in her tail.

Even on the bitterest of nights this endless winter, the one thing that got her up was the sound of my car pulling into the driveway. Her little face would appear in the dining room window by the time I reached the front door. She always greeted me with a grin, even as her legs collapsed beneath her.

She loves me, I'm sure, but her heart belongs to my husband. She has never had to struggle to the window to greet him. For him, she sits there from the moment he leaves the house, her patience reflected in her liquid brown eyes as she stares at the empty driveway. Her tail begins thumping on the floor before his car even makes the turn onto our street.

In January, when she stopped getting up, we began the conversation.

How long should we let this go on, I'd ask.

I don't know, he'd say.

I don't want her in pain, I'd say.

I don't either, he'd say. I love her so much.

How long. How long can we hold onto her.

I bought her non-skid booties so that, when she did gain her feet, she'd be less likely to slip on our wood floors.

Riley, our shepherd, groomed her. He spent his evenings licking her ears, her mouth, her body. When he finished, he'd lie down and gaze at her. How long.

My husband cleared paths in the yard so she wouldn't have to balance on a mound of frozen snow while she squatted. Still, he had to

*'How do you bring yourself to put a dog down
when she's lost only her legs
but still has her wag and her grin.'*

support her, turning his head away so as not to embarrass her.

One bitter cold night toward the end of January, he carried her to the yard and set her down as usual. She collapsed in his arms. He could not get her up. She wet her bed that night.

My husband took her to the vet in the morning. Is there anything more, anything at all we can do for her? He asked about adaquan, a drug that lubricates the joints. Sometimes it helps, the vet said. Often it doesn't. Let's try, my husband said.

And Scout chased a squirrel this morning.

There was a time when she might have caught it. When Scout was young, my boys used to race her down the street on their bicycles. She grinned into the wind, her ears flying, her legs churning. We'd have bet on her in a field of greyhounds.

This morning, there was no sign of that long-ago racer. She was so slow, so awkward. She lost her footing a couple of times.

No matter. Scout was chasing a squirrel. She chugged along over patches of leftover snow. The squirrel watched her progress with disdain, then finally ceded the contest and climbed to the top of the fence.

Scout was satisfied. The grin never left her face as she turned and cautiously made her way back to the house.

We have bought time. I don't know how much. I will be surprised if she makes it through another winter. I am hoping that her good heart gives out in her sleep before her legs completely fail her. I am hoping she does us that great favor. I am hoping.

Because how do you bring yourself to put a dog down when she's lost only her legs but still has her wag and her grin.

Scout 2003

Scout 2003

Requiem
for the Little Brown Dog

Scout, our little brown dog, is gone.

She died last Sunday at the age of 12½.

I wrote about her failing health a few weeks ago. After that column ran, I had so many calls and notes from readers who had concern and advice to offer.

I appreciated them all. But there were two pieces of advice that stood out for me:

Do not pre-mourn her. Live each day that you have with her as she lives − in the moment.

We did. My husband and I took that advice to heart and stopped seeing a dead dog every time we looked at her. We saw our Scout and were grateful.

The other bit of advice helped in the end. Listen to the dog, someone said. She will tell you when it is time.

She did.

It was a ruptured disk that paralyzed her. She walked her last steps Friday, in the middle of the night. She was trying to get outside through the dog door. The noise of the door flapping, again and again, was what woke me. I found her with her head poking out. Her body would not follow. I carried her to the yard.

On Saturday, as Scout lay serenely on her bed, Bob and I allowed ourselves to understand what she already knew. She would never again chase a bug − one of her all-time favorite sports. She would never again catch a snowball. She would never again have control of her bladder. She knew. And she accepted.

Riley, our shepherd, spent Saturday lying in front of Scout. Occasionally, he got up to lick her face, her ears, her eyes. Riley knew, too. His best pal would never again be rising from her bed to steal his chewie away.

That, too, was among her favorite pastimes. As weak as her hind legs were, she had done it Thursday night. She waited until Riley was out of the room, then walked the 10 feet to where his chewie lay. She took it back to her bed, placing it carefully before her to await his discovery of her subterfuge.

*'And so I held her in my arms
while Bob stroked her beautiful little
face. She was gone in a matter of seconds.'*

What could be better than to still be capable of taunting Riley? It was a wonderful game.

When Riley discovered the theft, he stood before her crying. At twice her size, he would never have considered stealing it back. I intervened to retrieve it for him.

We took her Sunday morning. Our vet offered to come to the house, but we said no. Neither of us was sure we could possibly face being with her in the end. We feared our own cowardice.

My husband carried her into the office and laid her gently on the stainless steel table. And we realized immediately that we had to stay. The only alternative was to let Scout watch us turn away and walk out on her. I couldn't bear knowing that our backs would be the last image she had of us. Neither could Bob.

And so I held her in my arms while Bob stroked her beautiful little face. She was gone in a matter of seconds.

I know many people who have been through this pain. Some find it so terrible that they protect themselves from the prospect of facing it again by never getting another dog.

We are not among them. We will do it again. And again. There is never a happy ending when you have a dog. Dogs die. But we would not deny ourselves the joy and the laughter and the friendship that a dog brings into our family. We might as well not live at all if we avoid love out of fear of inevitable loss.

Riley is desolate. He lies on Scout's bed for long hours, moving only the tip of his tail when we try to console him. Dogs are unable to comfort themselves by finding distractions, keeping busy. He will feel what he feels until he feels something else.

He will soon need a new pal. He will need a puppy to train just as Scout trained him – one who will eventually grieve for him just as he now grieves for Scout.

We will, too. Not today. Not next week. But soon.

Meanwhile, there is a shadow over our house. Our Scout is gone. We loved her so much.

Bob Quinn

Tom, Huck and grandpups Little Mac and Gus with Beth and Melissa 2005

The Vicious Poodle
of Park Avenue

Note: *As you read earlier in this book, my son Sean became popular during a summer job as a doorman on Park Avenue due to having a family dog who was taken out by the mob.*

In this story, a different dog was responsible for his rise to hero status on that same New York street.

This is the story of how a poor college boy became a hero on Park Avenue.

The college boy belongs to me. He is mine, and the main result of this is that I pay his annual eleven-million-dollar tuition. But I am reasonably poor, and so he works three jobs during the summer to help pay his diploma's ransom.

One of his jobs is that of doorman on Park Avenue in New York City. Opening doors is a nuisance for the people who live on Park Avenue, so they pay others to dress up in uniforms and do the door opening on their behalf.

As it happens, a dog named Homer lives in this Park Avenue building, and he doesn't like opening doors any better than the people do.

Homer is a black poodle. With a name like Homer, you'd think he might be like a regular guy poodle, but Homer is too wealthy to be a regular guy. He's fairly big as poodles go – perhaps 50 or 60 pounds – but any chance he might have had of being a regular guy has been ruined by the red velvet bow that his Mistress makes him wear on his head.

Homer spends a good deal of time at his hairdresser, having perms and trims and such. In fact, the word among the doormen is that Homer's beauty parlor tab is $300 a week – and that doesn't include the cost of the limo that drives him there and back. My boy opens the limo door for Homer on these occasions.

Homer knows his rank, which is way above that of doorman. And to remind the doormen of this, Homer has developed the habit of biting them, usually in their Vulnerable Spot, if you get my meaning.

Naturally none of the doormen like getting bit by Homer because, in addition to the pain it causes, they fear it could cost them their jobs if they react poorly to it. In fact, the career doormen gave my boy a piece of advice should he have the misfortune of getting bit by Homer.

"If Homer bites you, it's your fault," they told him. "Apologize to him."

But weeks went by without Homer biting my boy. On beauty parlor days, Homer sometimes made a half-hearted pass at him as he entered the limo, but he didn't seem to have the interest to get behind a good bite.

In fact, Homer was so indifferent to my boy that it began to seem he might make it through the summer without getting bit. But his luck ran out last week when Homer's Mistress returned from a holiday.

"Take this luggage," Homer's Mistress told my boy. And so he loaded his arms with the first half dozen or so of her suitcases, and they entered her private elevator.

Just knowing his arms were full and his Vulnerable Spot was unprotected caused my boy to break out in a sweat.

Homer was waiting for them in the foyer. He greeted his Mistress, then turned his attention to my boy. It was clear, said my boy, that Homer was sizing up the opportunity.

The Mistress walked on ahead, summoning my boy toward her bedroom suite. He followed closely, keeping Homer in the corner of his eye as he staggered along with the suitcases. And Homer kept my boy in the corner of his own eye as he edged along with him.

It happened in the bedroom, just as the Mistress went into a closet. Homer saw his chance and, as his Mistress disappeared, he lunged for my boy's Vulnerable Spot.

My boy saw him coming, and without his meaning for it to happen, he suddenly threw all six suitcases into the air. They went flying around the room a bit, and then crashed into some Louie the Fourteenth armoires and other such furniture. But the crashing didn't faze Homer. He kept coming for the Vulnerable Spot, growling in his throat and baring his teeth.

Just as he was about to take his bite, my boy bent down, scooped the growling Homer up in his arms and then he … well, he didn't know what to do with him because Homer wouldn't quit thrashing around and growling. So, without meaning to, he threw him at one of the Louie the Fourteenth things.

Homer landed on it with a thud. Then he and the Louie the Fourteenth thing crashed backward into the wall.

Grandpup Gus with Sean 1998

It was over in five seconds. My boy couldn't believe he had done it. Neither could Homer.

The dog was unhurt, but it was clear by the look of him that he'd had a misadventure. His perm was disheveled and his red velvet bow hung cockeyed over one ear. He sat leaning against the wall, staring stupidly at my boy.

As for my boy, he stood in the center of the room staring stupidly at the Louie the Fourteeth things that Homer and the suitcases had crashed into.

It was then, of course, that the Mistress came out of the closet. She surveyed the mess.

"I … uh … I apologized to Homer," my boy told the Mistress. There seemed nothing else for him to say.

"Well, then," she said, and, to my boy's great surprise, the matter was closed.

Homer, however, will be awhile getting over the incident. He haughtily ignores my boy now whenever he goes to the hairdresser.

As for the doormen, they have told the story among their ranks up and down Park Avenue.

"He threw Homer!" they tell each other, and then they come around to slap my boy on the back and hear the tale firsthand.

And that is how a poor college boy became a hero on Park Avenue.

The Adventures of Huckleberry Quinn

By Huck Quinn

I am Huckleberry, the new puppy living in the house with Beth Quinn and Bob and Riley.

I am a chocolate Lab and I am told I am going to get medicated soon with calm-down pills as I am very, very busy, yes, yes, too busy, too too too busy.

I have a lot of energy, yes, yes, yes, and – take right now, right now I need a chewie, need a chewie, oh boy oh boy oh boy oh boy!!! I have to take the chewie –Delish! – out through the dog door, yes yes, to the garden to bury it! I have to dig, dig …

Oh ho! what's this, what's this, a flower Bob planted, yes! He put it in, I take it out, division of labor, yes! and I drag it in through the dog door and put it where? put it where? I know, put it on the bed, yes yes! It looks good with the dirt on the bed!

I hear water! what's going on with water in the bathroom, water running behind the curtain because I am a water dog, yes! so I have to get into the water and, wait, wait!! I will bring the toilet paper into the water, too!!

And uh oh! it's Beth Quinn's water, she's in the shower too with me! We're in the water together!!!! Oh oh oh oh oh!! it's soap! I have to eat the soap – Delish! – and take it and run out of the shower and shake and shake and shake the water off me all over the pile of clean towels!!

And wait, the soap has to go here, here! with the plant on the bed!! Oooh and I'm slippery, sliding on the floor and crashing into the nightstand with the alarm clock and – uh oh! – crash it comes down!!!

Good grief good grief good grief!! here comes Riley, big shepherd Riley! He's German, I'm Labradorian, he has rules, I'm like a drunken sailor, yes!!! I'll sit, sit! 'til he goes by. He doesn't approve of me, he stares and has rules! and he doesn't run and dig and get in the shower, no!

I need a plan, yes, a plan to get something else for the pile on the bed! and I think I'll get the dish towel now in the kitchen and … holy cow!!! what's that on the counter!! I must jump up, jump up to

Huck and Riley 2003

'And uh oh uh oh uh oh Ruley Riley
coming out the dog door to see Bob and lick his toe
and sit on my head because
I am a drunken Labradorian sailor!!!!'

see if it's meat because it is! it is! it's meat! and I have to take it, take it down to the cellar and eat it behind the dryer – Delish! – and

Holy mackerel!!!!!! – what's this, a knee-hi stocking on the back of the dryer where the lint comes out!!! I need the knee-hi!!! and I must take it to the living room and get on the couch and shake and shake and shake the lint everywhere and then eat it – Delish! – and then puke!!!!

We need a log, yes a log in the house, a fireplace log, I have to go out the dog door – wait! wait! I have to take the couch pillow out the dog door with me and and and and – I know, I know! – I have to put the pillow in the little swimming pool, yes! and now the log, yes oooh oooh oooh heavy dragging the log to the dog door to get it inside and

… ooommph!!!! … sideways doesn't work through the dog door!!! Leave it here, yes here by the dog door oooh oooh oooh here comes Bob out the dog-door door and Yeeooow!!! his toe his toe his toe on the log! He's hopping on one leg because his toe, and I'm jumping too too too!!!

And uh oh uh oh uh oh Ruley Riley coming out the dog door to see Bob and lick his toe and sit on my head because I am a drunken Labradorian sailor!!!!

Hide in the house, yes! hide hide under the computer and see this?? see this??? see this?!?!?!? it's a computer cord yes!!! to the mouse – Delish! –and Beth Quinn says don't don't don't don't!!! and I pull and she says stop stop stop!!! because she won't be able to write any-mo

Right-Wing Puppy Politics

I lent my dog-training bible, "Good Owners, Great Dogs," to my friend Jim. Jim's a wise guy, and when he saw the title he concluded that the book's authors must be liberals because "they obviously want us to take care of our dogs."

He wanted the right-wing Republican training book.

"I want a dog who will take care of himself and not come whining to me every time he needs something," Jim told me.

It occurred to me there might be a niche for such a thing. It would certainly be a different approach to pet care. So I've decided to do it here, in our first installment of:

Ask A Right-Wing Republican
(No more Molly-Coddling!)

Dear Right-Wing Republican: My dog Zelda keeps having one litter of pups after another. She's just such a wanton, little minx! Can you offer any guidance?

Dear Zelda's Owner: Teach Zelda to "just say no"! If she doesn't, well … she made her bed, now she'll just have to lie in it.

Dear Right-Wing Republican: Health insurance rates for my Seeing Eye dog Bruce have gone through the roof, and I can no longer afford it. I can't get group rates because there's just Bruce working for me. Any suggestions?

Dear Bruce's Owner: Reduce Bruce's workload to 30 hours a week. That way, he's a part-time worker and you're under no obligation to offer him benefits!

Dear Right-Wing Republican: My dog Malcolm seems to have an amorous attachment to our other dog, Jasper. In addition, he's enormously attracted to the legs of our male visitors, if you know what I'm saying. Do you think Malcolm is gay?

Dear Malcolm's Owner: Perversions like Malcolm's must be wiped out. Dogs aren't born gay; they choose to be gay. They must be taught to change their sinful ways. Get thee to a deprogrammer.

Tom 2004

'*Dear Right-Wing Republican:*
My dog Malcolm seems to have
an amorous attachment to our other dog,
Jasper. Do you think Malcolm is gay?'

Dear Right-Wing Republican: We have a stray dog in the neighborhood who I'd like to help, but every time I approach, he runs away. Do you have any advice?

Dear Bleeding Heart Dope: What do you care? It's a dog's own fault if he's homeless! He's probably lazy and has no self-respect. Filthy habits, too, no doubt! If he starts stealing food, perhaps the police can be called to throw him in the pound.

Dear Right-Wing Republican: We'd like to adopt a dog from a shelter, but we're not sure which shelter might be best. Do you have any guidelines?

Dear Dog-less: As you may know, we oppose government funding for any shelter that "fixes" dogs or otherwise engages in family planning activities. We have a plan to provide funding for religious shelters, however, where dogs can learn good morals while the do gooders feed them. Seek a moral shelter to find a dog with good family values.

Dear Right-Wing Republican: When I walk my dog Dog in our local park, he likes to dig up flower beds, chase squirrels and leave a "mess" behind, if you get my meaning. Can you suggest a way to break him of these habits?

Dear Dog's Owner: It's incumbent upon us all to maintain our park lands in pristine and unsullied condition and to preserve our flora and fauna for all Americans to enjoy in their natural habitat.

When Dog starts digging … hey, wait a minute! Do you think there might be oil under your park? If so, have we got a job for Dog!

The Curious Case
of the Ghost in the Night

The night the flashlight turned on by itself was when I fully realized that I'm a ninny. It was also the night I conceded that my son, Brendan, was right 20 years ago when he said a ghost lived in our wicker trunk.

It happened three weeks ago, on one of those dark and windy nights that, in the movies, comes with banging shutters and creaking stairs. I always shout "Get out!" to the people in those movies, but they never listen. Instead, they "go investigate."

I'm no investigator. Mainly, when I hear a banging shutter, I just lie in bed with the covers to my chin and my eyes popped wide open.

On the night the flashlight turned itself on, I was alone in the house except for our two Lab puppies – Tom and Huck Quinn.*

As puppies go, they're more entertaining than nitrous oxide, but as guard dogs they're about as useless as a spare appendix.

I don't know whether it was the wind or my bladder that woke me up at 4:30 in the morning. I untangled myself from the pups, which was no mean trick. Huck was curled up in the crook of my legs and Tom lay spread-eagle on his back with his head on Huck's belly. They were oblivious to both the weather and me.

I got up and padded to the bathroom. But I stopped moving mid-pad when I got a look at the bathroom window. It was suffused with an eerie glow, which was emanating from the porch.

Well, I couldn't imagine why my porch was glowing in the middle of the night, so I did the only logical thing I could think of. I went back to the bedroom and woke up the pups. I didn't want to be alone at a time like this.

"Huck," I said. "Wake up, Huck."

To her credit, she popped right up, smiling and wagging. Then she jumped off the bed and found a ball in the corner of the room. Huck never lets an opportunity to play a little ball go by.

*For those who've been following the life and times of my dogs, our shepherd Riley died shortly after we lost Scout, our little brown dog. I didn't write about it and won't. It's one sad dog story too many.

Huck and Tom 2003

'I carried Tom, asleep on my shoulder,
to the porch door.
Huck pranced behind me with the ball in her mouth.
We were pretty much prepared for a game of fetch
or a pee pee in the back yard,
but we were ill-equipped for combating an eerie glow.'

I shook Tom to get him going. Tom is the laziest puppy I've ever known, and waking him up is a full-time job. He needs a good, long spell of stretching and yawning before he comes to.

I didn't have time to wait, though, so I grabbed him up in my arms and headed for the porch. In retrospect, I realize this was a foolish thing to do. A sleeping puppy is a poor talisman against an eerie glow.

Even so, I carried Tom, asleep on my shoulder, to the porch door. Huck pranced behind me with the ball in her mouth. We were pretty much prepared for a game of fetch or a pee pee in the back yard, but we were ill-equipped for combating an eerie glow.

As soon as I stepped onto the porch, I saw my flashlight on the shelf. It was on! Somehow it had come to life! A serial killer must have switched on the light and then hid on the premises just waiting for his chance!

Naturally, the idea of a serial killing flashlight-lighter scared me silly. I hauled Tom back to the bedroom and snatched up my only weapon, a Louisville slugger, which I keep by the bed for just such eventualities.

So now I was holding a sleeping puppy and a baseball bat. Huck grew excited at the prospect of a full-blown ball game. She began springing on and off the bed like a crazed short stop.

Well, that's when the ninny in me took over. Instead of searching for the killer, I put Tom back to bed, got the ball away from Huck and crawled under the covers. I stared wide-eyed at the ceiling until dawn, trying to figure out the meaning of the night's proceedings.

And then it hit me. This was no serial killer. I had let the ghost loose.

It was the puppies' fault, really. They'd chewed up the ghost's wicker trunk, and I'd finally put it out with the garbage. That very day, in fact! The ghost was obviously trying to bring attention to its plight.

I called my son for a consultation. After all, it was Brendan's ghost. Or it used to be. He was only 10 when he'd found it, but now that he's grown up he's forgotten. That happens sometimes, and it's a damn shame.

But I'm sticking with my theory. After all, a ghost is better than a serial killer. Plus, now I've got evidence.

I went and bought a new trunk for that ghost, and you know what? The flashlight hasn't lit up ever since.

A Midterm Report on the Puppyhood of Tom and Huck

There is a theory among those who enjoy the company of Labrador retrievers that their behavior is somehow directly linked to their color.

Black Labs are said to be the calmest and easiest to train. Yellows lie somewhere in the middle. And chocolates are both a bit on the frantic side and ... well ... not the sharpest knife in the drawer.

I find it hard to believe that there's a single gene in a dog that dictates, all in one shot, color, frenetic activity and a penchant for losing one's way. But empirical evidence in my own home suggests there might be some merit to the theory.

Huckleberry Quinn, our 10-month-old chocolate Lab, has a rather dangerous combination of traits: mild duncery and massive gusto.

Tom, our 5-month-old yellow, is deeply introspective, has a discerning wit and he maintains a rather come-what-may attitude toward the vagaries of life.

Consider their different responses when I take their leashes off the peg for the evening walk. Huck leans toward apoplexy:

HOLY CRAP!!! A WALK!!! WE'RE GOING FOR A WALK!!! HOLY CRAP!!! WE NEVER WENT FOR A WALK BEFORE!!!

Tom, who is equally glad to see the leashes come down, is nevertheless more inclined to take the momentous event in stride:

Well, isn't this just fabulous. A walk. Here, let me help with that leash by sitting still for you.

In the Obedience Category, I also find distinctions between chocolate and yellow.

In Huck's case, there is reason to believe that the dog has gone deaf. Our exchanges, as a consequence, tend to get a bit repetitive:

Sit, Huck.

Sit, Huck.

Sit, Huck, sit. Sit. Sit sit sit, Huck. SIT! FOR CRYING OUT LOUD, SIT THE HELL DOWN, HUCK!!!

Tom, observing my growing agitation, has long since sat even though his name isn't Huck.

In the Logic and Memorization Category, Tom also has the upper hand. Consider Huck's failure to grasp the fact that the neighbors *live* there.

She's been watching them come and go for months now, yet she persists in the belief that she must engage in loud reports about their activities.

Tom responds by cocking an ear, noting the make and model of their car and concluding that it doesn't require any further attention on his part.

It is in the Good Judgment Category, though, where the yellow is really separated from the chocolate.

Consider Huck's food choices: crayons, Ivory soap, logs, snow, ballet slippers, dish towels and flowers when in season.

Consider Tom's food choices: food.

Consider, too, Huck's penchant for involving herself in my activities. She steals my toothbrush while I'm brushing my teeth, climbs into the fireplace while I'm lighting a fire and ... no, I won't go there. You don't want to know what she does while I'm on the toilet.

Tom, on the other hand, seems to respect my belongings and my privacy. And he has managed to discern, in his short five months of life, that fire is HOT.

I realize that not all yellow Labs are this mellow. Nor are all chocolate Labs this ... irregular. Suggesting otherwise would be dangerously akin to stereotyping. No doubt, your own chocolate Lab behaves splendidly.

But I fear the stereotype has taken hold in our own family. My son's yellow Lab, Gus, behaves much as Huck does. He once gave himself a concussion and perhaps a bit of brain damage – hard to tell – when he enthusiastically ran headlong into the side of a garage.

Given that Gus is yellow, you might fairly ask how this story perpetuates the stereotype that chocolates are the lunatics. I will tell you.

In our family, we refer to Gus as a yellow-coated chocolate Lab.

Huck 2003

'HOLY CRAP!!! A WALK!!!
WE'RE GOING FOR A WALK!!!
HOLY CRAP!!!
WE NEVER WENT FOR A WALK BEFORE!!!'

Night School
for Your 'Special' Dog

Once again, the Westminster dog show has put me mildly to shame.

I watched it last week with Tom and Huck, my two Labs.

There I was, admiring Carlee holding a "free stack," while Tom and Huck were holding a "free-for-all" in the living room. Neither they nor I had ever heard of a free stack.

In case you haven't either, it involves a dog standing still for a long time in a perfect pose. My dogs neither stand still nor do they pose at all.

In truth, it's my fault. Instead of training them, I've befriended them. I just can't bring myself to order my friends about. They might not like me anymore. What's a dog for, if not to like you?

But anyone who's pals with Labrador retrievers knows they really do need a bit of guidance. In general, they are, shall we say, a bit "special."

Forget about show-dog classes. The following is the kind of school we Friends Of The Lab need.

EVENING CLASSES FOR SPECIAL DOGS

Note: Because of the level of difficulty of the following courses, class size will be limited to four participants.

PUBLIC GROOMING
BODY PARTS YOU CAN CHEW ON IN FRONT OF CHURCH LADIES
Open forum.

ETIQUETTE
HOW TO GREET YOUR HUMANS AT THE DOOR
Video and role-playing.

THE NEIGHBORS
WHO ARE THEY, REALLY?
Roundtable discussion.

PSYCHOLOGY
LEARNING TO LIVE WITH THAT DESPICABLE CAT
Panel of experts discuss the psycho-social strategy of "ignore."

THE CAR
ARE YOU REALLY JUST SUPPOSED TO SIT THERE AND LOOK OUT THE WINDOW?
Driving simulation. (Note: Fee does not include insurance.)

HEALTH WATCH
NOT EVERYTHING IS FOOD
Real-life testimonial (via satellite from the hospital)
from one dog who didn't know that.

DECISION-MAKING
IS A FEATHER BED SOMETHING TO HAVE A TUG OF WAR WITH?
Debate.

FETCH
ACCEPTING THE FACT THAT THE BALL HAS BEEN PUT AWAY AND THE GAME IS OVER
Relaxation techniques, meditation.

FRIEND OR FOE
THE MAIL CARRIER VERSUS THE BURGLAR
Pictures, graphics.

PIDDLING
YOU'RE OLD ENOUGH NOW TO LIFT A LEG
For males only. Step-by-step slide presentation.

GETTING OVER IT
THE OPERATION WAS SUPPOSED TO MEAN
YOU WERE NO LONGER SEXUALLY ATTRACTED TO GUESTS' LEGS
Helpline, support group referrals included.

OUR HUMAN FUSSBUDGETS
THE DIFFERENCE BETWEEN THE TOILET AND THE WATER BOWL
Plenary session.

CHEWIES WILL BE SERVED!

Huck Reads the Stars for Your Dog

By Huck Quinn

Daily horoscopes aren't just for people. Read on and learn what's in store for your dog today.

★★ **ARIES (March 21-April 19):** When put on the spot, you will fail to remember what "Sit!" means. Avoid travel today; a gnat will fly into your mouth when you stick your head out the car window. To your dismay, your owner will take up the flute.

★ **TAURUS (April 20-May 20):** Do not trust the cat today; he will do something despicable and blame you. There is something in your yard that needs to be dug up immediately. Your nerves will be shot when the fire whistle goes off.

★★★★ **GEMINI (May 21-June 20):** Once again, you will not catch the squirrel. You will face a complicated dilemma when the UPS man arrives just as you realize you're thirsty. You will have an uncharitable thought about the children at the school bus stop.

★★ **CANCER (June 21-July 22):** You will make a funny sound, then your owner will announce it was you, not him. You attempt to watch Animal Planet but fall asleep before you find out what happened to the meerkat. It's time to stop living your life for others.

★★★★★ **LEO (July 23-Aug. 22):** Today is your lucky day! A child comes to visit and drops food on the floor. You will begin to scratch behind your ear, then realize it's your butt that's itchy. You bravely decide to take a nap on a different part of the rug.

★★ **VIRGO (Aug. 23-Sept. 22):** Your owner is right: You will never understand the meaning of "Stay!" You will discover that the man in your house, until now your ally, has learned to put the toilet lid down. Once again, your owner will feed the other dog first.

★ **LIBRA (Sept. 23-Oct. 22):** You will sprain something while attempting to leap onto the counter after the cat. You get the distinct feeling that your owner will never buy a different brand of dog food. Learn what b-a-t-h spells so there are no more surprises.

Huck 2003

★★★★ *AQUARIUS (Jan. 20-Feb. 18):*
This is an ideal time to change direction when you
circle three times before lying down.
The cat's lucky number is 9; yours is 10.

★★ **SCORPIO (Oct. 23-Nov. 21):** A sun spot will move while you are asleep. Long after the operation, you will come to terms with the fact that they will never grow back. When your owner tells you the steak is his, you will completely miss the point.

★★★ **SAGITTARIUS (Nov. 22-Dec. 21):** You will try to bring a long stick into the house through the dog door for several hours. You will make a discovery in the cat's litter box. You learn, to your chagrin, that yellow jackets do not respond well to being eaten.

★★ **CAPRICORN (Dec. 22-Jan. 19):** You feel amorous, but your owner will push you off his leg. You hear the call of the wild but don't want to miss dinner. You discover you have no aptitude for Frisbee. Unfortunately, you find a leftover Easter egg in the back yard.

★★★★ **AQUARIUS (Jan. 20-Feb. 18):** This is an ideal time to change direction when you circle three times before lying down. The cat's lucky number is 9; yours is 10. You will give your owner the cold shoulder when he makes you wear deer antlers and sunglasses.

★★ **PISCES (Feb. 19-March 20):** Explore your options; don't settle for a biscuit when liverwurst is available. You need a new strategy for getting the refrigerator door open. It's time to admit that you don't know whether you like the color red.

BORN TODAY: You are a miracle of apathy about politics. Your feelings about the cat will remain unchanged throughout your lifetime. You will discover early on that all you need is one good friend.

Huck Quinn's
Got a Tale to Tell

By Huck Quinn

I, Huckleberry Quinn, speakin' on behalf of myself, which is a 15-month-old chocolate Lab, and also on behalf of Tom, which is my best friend, him bein' a 10-month-old yellow Lab which does not have such good command of the language yet, do hereby give the followin' account of the incident involvin' the tennis ball and the broken things.

Me and him didn't mean no harm by it, really, and it was him, meanin' Tom, which started the situation, but I ain't tryin' to make him take the blame. I went along, I won't lie about that.

But Tom, he had a powerful urge to get aholt of that tennis ball, which was lyin' outa reach behind the rocking chair on the side porch, which is where me and him pass the time while the adults are away from the house at work and such.

He worried over that ball for more'n an hour or so, give or take (I'm not yet acquainted with the workins of a clock), hunkerin' down on the floor in front of that rocker and pokin' one leg in and then another as though one a them might be longer 'n the other if only he could just figure out which one was the long one.

Then he'd give up on that for awhile and squish his face against the floor with one eye all crinkled up in the cement tiles and stare at that ball and have hisself a good cry.

I told him, I sez Tom, you might just as well quit because that ball ain't gettin' any closer, but he had no regard for my advice and he just kept starin' and pokin' at it.

I started feelin' real sorry for him.

Truth be told, I started wantin' that ball myself. It was a well-seasoned ball, one of them tennis balls that's had just the right amount of chew done on it so's it's got some roughness to its surface. So I got to thinkin' and by 'n by I struck on an idea of my own about how to get to it.

I recalled that our Mama sometimes uses a yardstick to get balls out of stuck places, and I knew just where she kept that yardstick – on a hook at the top of the cellar steps, right there next to the mop and the broom and a big ole bag filled with other bags and the fly swatter and just about everything in the house that can be hung up.

So I told Tom, I sez we gotta' go get that yardstick that Mama uses to get our balls outa tight spots. And Tom, he perked right up and followed me over to the top of the cellarway.

It took two of us workin' together to pull down that yardstick. And the mop. And the broom. And the bag of bags and the fly swatter. I tell you, when they all went clatterin' down the stairs like that into the dark below I about jumped right outa my fur I was so scairt, and Tom, he went flyin' out the dog door into the yard, cryin' like the baby he is. I never seen him so scairt 'cept that time he came face to face with a skunk, but that is another story.

I coulda' gone down the cellar and got the yardstick, I guess, but my nerves were wore out what with all that hollerin' comin' from Tom, so I went out to see if I could get him to quit before he upset the whole neighborhood. And it was then I spied the wisteria tree and got the idea about usin' one of them branches to get the ball out from underneath the rocking chair.

So I told Tom, I sez let's see if we can pull one a them branches off that tree there and use that on the ball. And he quit his snivelin' and set to work right beside me – Tom might be a crybaby but I'll say this for him, he's strong as a ox – and we musta' pulled and pulled for an hour, give or take, until we got us a branch. I don't know how big it was, but from what I heard in the previous testimony given here today, I 'spect it was about eight feet long.

We rested for a bit after that while I considered how we might get that branch in through the dog door and onto the porch. I never did come up with a good plan so we just tried rammin' it through a few hunnert times or so until we got the angle right. I regret what it did to the siding on the house, as I already told our Mama.

Anyhow, once we got one end of it started into the dog door, I jumped ahead and pulled while Tom pushed from the other side, until we had that tree branch all the way into the porch. I know we shoulda never done that, but I can't say I'm too sorry. It was no easy trick.

I guess Tom was as proud as I was about our accomplishment because he just wanted to carry that branch around on the porch like he was some kinda prince. So he picked it up in his mouth and trotted this way and that, prancin' up and down like he was in a parade,

Bob Quinn

Tom and Huck 2005

'I told him, I sez Tom, you might just as well quit
because that ball ain't gettin' any closer,
but he had no regard for my advice.'

shakin' his head left and right and turnin' in circles.

That right there would account for what happened to the lamp and the fan and all them little knicky knacky things on the shelf like them photographs and them little candle holders and that little stereo Mama had out there.

Like I said, I wasn't the one what did it, but it was my idea to bring in the branch and I'm ownin' up to it.

Anyhow we never did get that tennis ball out from under the rocker. But once Tom got hisself done with wreckin' the place, we went on outside again and found our spare balls in the garden and then we spent the remainder of our day runnin' around the yard with them two balls in our mouths.

They wasn't nearly as tasty as that tennis ball, though, but that don't matter none. That ball's still in the porch there, behind the rocker. I 'spect we'll have another go at it by 'n' by.

Huck Quinn's Advice to the Class of 2005

By Huck Quinn

Speaking strictly as a dog, there's not a lot of wisdom in taking time out from a squeaky toy to write a commencement speech about wisdom. The truly wise simply live wisely and don't talk much about it.

Even so, it's been my observation in my two years as a dog that certain rules of conduct apply equally to dogs and humans.

And so, upon request, I have agreed to pass on a few rules of dewclaw to those who are about to leave their litters and embark upon life in an uncertain world.

➤ Always choose the second-most comfortable chair. If you choose the best chair, someone will make you move.

➤ Have some pride. Don't beg.

➤ A handshake is the proper greeting. Don't sniff someone's butt. Things will get off to a bad start.

➤ Don't stand up in a moving vehicle.

➤ Pace yourself. Periods of high activity should be followed by a nap.

➤ If you have to puke, get off the rug.

➤ Don't whine. If you do, someone will eventually just tell you to "quit whining."

➤ Show a deep interest in what others are doing. For example, if someone likes gardening, GET INVOLVED. Help dig. If someone is sleeping, sleep right along with him.

➤ Be friendly.

➤ If you put your head out the car window, keep your mouth shut.

➤ Remember: Give others privacy in the bathroom. It's OK, though, to lie down in front of the door until they come out. (Also, there's no secret exit from the bathroom, so whoever went in will eventually come out. See "Don't whine.")

➤ Never eat a stick.

➤ It's more important to be nice than to be rich – as long as there's enough money for Greenies.

Tom 2003

'If you have to puke, get off the rug.'

➤ Bees are not meant to be toyed with.

➤ It is good to take walks, greet the neighbors, then go back home where you belong.

➤ Avoid having a whole litter of children. If you do, someone might sell them.

➤ Never chase cars.

➤ Hot air balloons probably won't harm you, but why take the chance? Go to the basement if one comes by.

➤ Be yourself. A pretentious dog – or person – is a laughingstock.

➤ Sit in the shade.

➤ Once in a while, run real fast for no reason.

➤ Don't eat soap. (See item on "puking.")

➤ Try not to let others choose your mate for you.

➤ Don't take yourself too seriously, but if you have a job, such as keeping an eye on the squirrel, take your work seriously.

➤ Don't hold a grudge. (A little sulking behind the shed is OK.)

➤ If someone comes home late, be happy to see him.

➤ In Frisbee, what matters the most is really wanting to catch it.

➤ Be humble. If you're not, others will just say, "He sure does think he's something, doesn't he," and then you're automatically not something anymore.

➤ Be careful around people with crutches.

➤ Never sneak sips from someone's beer glass. It catches up with you.

➤ In a pinch, if you feel confused, sit.

➤ Try not to knock stuff off the coffee table. It's upsetting and makes everyone have to get up for paper towels.

➤ And this above all: Give those you love a sloppy kiss at every opportunity.

Of course, if you're anything like a dog, you'll ignore the rules now and then if you don't happen to feel like following them on a particular day. That's fine, too. Just know that, if you do, someone will make you sit in the crate for a little timeout while you "think about what you did."

If that happens, don't forget to bring your squeaky toy. It makes the time go by.

He Who Lies with Dogs Gets no Sleep

Anyone who has shared the family bed with a dog knows the Law of Weights and Measures that says this: The deeper a dog sleeps, the heavier he becomes.

A dog that weighs 80 pounds awake and alert weighs 360 pounds by the time he reaches the deepest level of sleep. During REM sleep, when he is dreaming, he weighs a bit less but makes up for it by kicking you in the belly as he runs in his sleep.

In our house, Tom and Huck share the bed with my husband and me. An aerial view of us would reveal a mélange of dog legs and human arms jutting out from a central heap, a giant amoeba that mutates in form as the parts shift position through the night.

Except Tom. Our 80-pound yellow Lab doesn't shift. Tom settles into the center of the pile and the rest of us shift around him.

Tom is perhaps the most relaxed animal I've ever had occasion to share a bed with. He goes from "awake" to "coma" in the time it takes the rest of us to stake out our positions. When he jumps onto the bed for the night, he doesn't do settling-in things like most dogs and humans. No turning three times, no plumping of the pillows, no arranging of the covers.

Tom just collapses where he lands, stretched full out at whatever angle suits – horizontally, vertically or, most often, perpendicular to the rest of the crowd with his body bisecting everyone's side of the bed.

He's like a college lad who crashes after having too much to drink at the party, entirely unaware of what's going on around him. I could paint his face and he wouldn't notice.

What's going on around him, of course, is my husband, our choco-late Lab, Huck, and I trying to stake a little claim to the bed. Bob and I wrestle with the covers while Huck hovers at the foot of the bed waiting for everyone to settle in before finding her own spot.

All tossing and turning and shoving of Tom is usually to no avail. He is a lump of gravity. And as the night progresses, he steals even more space. He inches his way to dead center, claiming an inch here, a yard there, until I awaken to find myself gripping the edge of the

Huck and Tom 2003

*'In our house, Tom and Huck share the bed
with my husband and me. An aerial view
of us would reveal a mélange of dog legs
and human arms jutting out from a central heap,
a giant amoeba that mutates in form
as the parts shift position through the night.'*

mattress and the hem of the sheet.

"Move, Tom," I say with all the command I can muster, but I know it is pointless. Getting Tom to move means getting out of bed, grabbing him by the hind legs and hauling his body to a new spot. He barely notices, yet by the time I sprint to my side of the bed and jump into my newly created area, he's already rolled over and reclaimed it.

He snores and snorts and – most often when his hiney is positioned north and he has a direct shot at my face – he passes gas.

I doubt getting a larger bed would improve the situation. Even in a bed the size of an aircraft carrier, he would still want to be lumped up with us.

I've tried creating a sidecar for him by moving an old sea chest (with a cushion on top, of course) right next to the bed. But even if he's willing to start the night there, he eventually rises as if from the dead and descends on our legs.

Huck, on the other hand, is a strangely delightful bed companion. Her 70-pound body seems to levitate in sleep, hovering just above the covers so she doesn't crowd anyone out or cause inconvenience. She's sensitive, even in deep sleep, to our own restless movements, and she rises as we reposition ourselves around Tom until everyone is resettled. Then she curls into whatever space is available.

But she makes up for her nocturnal thoughtfulness when the sun rises. It is Huck who considers it her responsibility to get us up in the morning at whatever hour her body clock tells her the night has ended and it's time to RISE AND SHINE.

She begins by pawing the covers off me. If that fails, she nuzzles her head down deep into my neck. This is loving and sweet, but it gets fur stuck to my lips.

In the end, if I persist in at least feigning sleep, she sneezes on my face. I am awake.

For his part, Tom has to be shaken awake in the morning. He lifts his head and opens one eye in dull comprehension that it's time to end the sleep party and go our separate ways. Huck, meanwhile, has already taken a pee, found a tennis ball and is filling out the team line-up form for a baseball game.

I know that those who don't live with dogs – and even some who do – find all of this entirely preposterous. Why put up with it? Why not relegate the dogs to the floor? They're just dogs, for cryin' out loud.

Well, it beats me. There is much logic in what they say.

What I do know, though, is that when I come half-awake in the night and stretch out an arm to find a dog to hug, my world is good.

Hank Werkman

Beth and her sister Kris with Mike 1958

Beth Quinn has been with the Times Herald-Record in Middletown, N.Y., since 1982. In addition to writing a weekly opinion column, she is currently the paper's health editor.

Her work has appeared in publications ranging from the *Chicken Soup for the Soul* books and *Reader's Digest* to the *Sporting News* and *Dog Fancy.* She is also the author of *The Best of Beth,* a collection of her earlier columns.

She lives in Orange County with her husband, Bob Quinn. In addition to the dogs, they have two sons, Sean and Brendan; a daughter-in-law, Melissa; and a grandson, Sam.

Huck and Tom 2004